# IF I COULD ONLY WRITE A LINE

*The Religious and Inspirational Poetry Of Mary Southers*

*Selected & Edited by Charles C. Hagan, Jr.*

*IF I COULD ONLY WRITE A LINE*

Copyright © 2008 Charles C. Hagan, Jr.

All rights reserved. No part of this book may be used or reproduced in any manner whatsoever without the written permission of the publisher, except for the use of brief quotations embodied in critical articles and reviews.
Printed in the United States of America. For information address
Millennium Vision Press, 401 W. Main Street #706
Louisville, KY 40202

Interior design and typesetting by Jason F. Hickman.
Front and back cover design by Unique Cover Designs.com

**ISBN 978-0-9759490-1-6**
Library of Congress Control Number: **2004109658**

1. American Poetry-Afro American Authors 2. African American Authors 3. African American Poetry

First Printing November 2008

**THE POETRY OF MARY SOUTHERS**

**DEDICATED TO**

*Mary Southers*

*Shirley Gray, my deceased cousin
& Lester Crayton, my good friend
Paul J. Mullins, my law partner,
Karl E. Wilson Jr., godson
all who were both instrumental
in helping read, organize, and type these poems*

*Christopher M. Parker, my grandfather
and Florence Parker, my grandmother*

*Chris toper Hagan and Hubert Hagan, my brothers*

### *IF I COULD ONLY WRITE A LINE*

## ABOUT THE EDITOR

Charles C. Hagan, Jr. has been a practicing attorney in Louisville, KY for 29 years. He is a member of the Louisville and Kentucky Bar Associations, and is licensed to practice before the United States Supreme Court. He received his B.A. degree from the University of Louisville (1972) and his J.D. degree from the Brandeis School of Law in 1975. He is a former Upward Bound and CLEO student, and recieved the prestigous Earl Warren Legal Training Fellowship for three years while a law student. He practices law with Paul J. Mullins and concentrates in the areas of criminal defense, personal injury, and family law. He lives in Louisville, KY with two of his three sons.

## OTHER BOOKS BY CHARLES C. HAGAN, JR.

A Funny Thing Happened
On The Way To the Watergate,
by Charles C. Hagan Jr. and Richard N. Adams
(1972) privately published

&

Not Guilty Every Time - Keys To Courtroom Victory
Millennium Vision Press, Louisville, KY 2004
ISBN 0-9759490-0-4
Available through Amazon.com
or through Millennium Vision Press,
401 W. Main St. #706 Louisville, KY 40202
for $21.95 (includes shipping costs).

*THE POETRY OF MARY SOUTHERS*

## CONTENTS
## BOOK I

Prologue   7

About Mary Southers   8

If I Could Only Write A Line   10

Chapter One
**PRAISE GOD**   11
    Worship, Your Gift, Eminence, The Elevation,
    What Shall I Offer Thee, Oh Hail to the King,
    Aspiration, To Close The House of God,
    One Morning After Church, The Bells On Sunday Morning,
    The Good Old-Fashioned Way Oh, We of Little Faith

Chapter Two
**CHRIST OUR LORD**   23
    Come and Follow Me, The Father's Love, The Truth Shall Live,
    His Eyes, He Knows All About Us, As Unto Him,
    The Wounded Savior, In Bethlehem, Temptation Conquered,
    Jesus Is There, Carrying Christ, Crowns, Our Guide, God Our King,
    He Has Risen, I'm Always Near, For Me He Came,
    I Know Jesus and He Knows Me,
    Over Two Thousand Years Ago, The Babe of Bethlehem,
    He Who Sees the Sparrow, Christ is Victory,
    That's The Way They Did Our Savior,

Chapter Three
**SOLDIERS AND ARMIES**   47
    No Unknown Soldier, The Unpayable Debt, Our Boys Prayer,
    The Weight of All Flesh, We Without Sons,
    An Unknown Soldier In Times Like These, God's Army,
    Soldiers of Christ, There's Another Army

*IF I COULD ONLY WRITE A LINE*

Chapter Four
**PRAYERS** 55
    God We Thank You, Travelers Morning Offering,
    Comfort, Our Master Is There, Learning Christ,
    My Prayer for Thee, They Belong To Thee,
    Bless Thou Me Oh Mother, Lo These Many Years,
    Jesus Help Me

Chapter Five
**LIFE'S PRACTICAL LESSONS** 65
    Wits End Corner, God Does Not Forget, A Clean Heart,
    The Science of Forgetting, Heart Tenants, Kindness, Sedative,
    Two Way Rule, Bread Upon the Waters,
    You'll Have To Do It or Make It, Live For Something, Oh Haste

Chapter Six
**MOTHERHOOD** 75
    Oh The Love of Mother, Mother On Calvary's Hill, My Mother, Dear Mother,
    Oh The Love of Mother, To My Son, Mother of Mine,
    As Granny Is Today, Just Took A Little Walk With the Lord,
    Mother Has Fallen Asleep

Chapter Seven
**FRIENDSHIP** 85
    The Friendly Street, Sometimes I Wonder Why, I Have A Friend,
    Love That Will Not Let Thee Go, Over All is Love, Somebody Knows,
    Sharing, Friendships Path

Chapter Eight
**HOLIDAYS & SEASONS** 93
    My New Year, At Easter, Gone But Not Forgotten
    Declaration Day, On Your Birthday, Happy Birthday, Father's Day,
    Another Thanksgiving Day, Thanksgiving Day, Nothing Under the Sun,
    Light of the World, Christmas Greeting, Winter World, Winter

Chapter Nine
**HOPE FOR TOMORROW** 105
    The Joys of Tomorrow, Water, Someday We'll Understand
    There Is A Home, When Will I Know, Strength To Bear,
    Cheer Up, Well Done, Happy at Last *(Mary's first poem)*

# THE POETRY OF MARY SOUTHERS

## *PROLOGUE*

The first poem by any African American is credited to Lucy Terry Prince. *Bars Fight* was written in 1746, but first published in 1865. America's first published African American author was Jupiter Hammond. He is credited with writing an 88-line broadside entitled *An Evening Thought: Salvation by Christ, with Penetential Cries* published in Hartford, Connecticut around 1760. The first book of poetry by an African American female was *Poems on Various Subjects Religions and Moral* by Phyllis Wheatley (1773). George Moses Horton (1797?-1883?) was the first Southern Black man to publish a volume of poetry in America, *The Hope of Liberty*, (1829). Ann Plato was the second woman of color to publish a book of essays and poems, *Essays*, (1841), and the first novel published by a black person in the United States was *Our Nig* by Harriet Wilson (1859).

The 18th and the 19th centuries were formidable periods in African American literary and cultural history. Prior to the civil war, the majority of Black Americans were held in bondage. Both law and practice forbade teaching Blacks to learn to read and write. However this did not stop them from learning to read and write prior to the end of slavery. Even after the war, many of the impediments to learning and literary productivity remained. "Nevertheless, Black men and women of the nineteenth century continued in their quest to learn to read and write". See, *African American Women Writers of the 19th Century* – The New York Public Library, Digital Library Collection, Digital Schomburg, copyright 1999.

Beginning in the 19th century African Americans published many dozens of volumes of poetry and thousands of individual poems. Yet few of their works are accessible today, and works by lesser-known black authors were generally overlooked. The problem in the search for Black women who wrote poetry in the 19th & 20th centuries is (1) identifying women who wrote poetry, (2) finding their published works, and (3) locating accurate biographical information. Many researchers have called them "invisible poets". They also say that these African American authors, men and women, had a poetic mastery of a great variety of subjects and styles, and a great range of poetic talent. It is with the above thoughts in mind that myself and my brothers have decided to publish the poetry of our great-grandmother, Mary Southers, written in the 1930's and 1940's. We pray that her poetry will inspire scholars and researchers to continue to study black men and women writers of the 18th and 19th centuries. Who know what gems and golden nuggets of literature may be found!

# IF I COULD ONLY WRITE A LINE

## ABOUT MARY SOUTHERS

Mary Southers was my great-grandmother and was born to John Hightower and Kitty (Taylor) Hightower on May 31, 1886 in Louisville, KY. Mary Southers had four sisters, Sallie, Bertha, Sophie and Lula. Her first marriage was to Neil Parker, a teamster and mechanic, who died at age 35 due to an accident. Neil and Mary had two sons, Christopher, and Clarence Parker. Mary later married Ike Southers and they had one son, Bert Southers. Kitty (Taylor) Hightower, and Bertha Hightower, her sister, are prominently mentioned as some of the early members of the Lampton Baptist Church, one of Louisville's oldest and most prestigious African American churches.

Mary Southers accepted Christ and joined the Lampton Baptist Church on February 28, 1896. She held her membership under the pastorate of three of Lampton's great leaders: Rev. C.C. Bates, Rev. J. M. Williams, and Dr. Charles H. Owens. In 1929 and at the age of 32, her son, Clarence Edward Parker, became one of the first African Americans motorcycle officers with the Louisville Police Department. Mary Southers lived most of her life in Louisville's east end at 718 Rear South Shelby Street. The occupation listed on her death certificate and census records is housekeeper. Even though we have attempted to learn from all available historical sources in the Louisville area, little is known about the early childhood, education, and life of Mary Southers. Mary Southers was 65 years of age when she died on March 17, 1951. She was funeralized at the Lampton Baptist Church, and was buried in the Louisville Cemetery.

Christopher M. Parker, Mary's oldest son, was my grandfather, and was born on March 9, 1909. He was married to Florence Parker, my grandmother. He died in January 1985. After his death me and my brothers, Christopher Hagan, and Hubert Hagan, were privileged to discover over 240 poems and writings written by Mary Southers. These poems were written in the 1930's and 1940's, and had been hidden away in an old trunk of my grandfather's since her death in 1951. To our knowledge, no one ever saw them after he took sole possession of them upon her death.

These poems are original, authentic, and were all written by hand by Mary Southers. All of the original writings still exist. To the best of our knowledge, these poems have never been published. Mary Southers often read some of these poems at church on different occasions. From her notes, it appears that she sent copies of poems to church members, relatives and friends and as thanksgiving gifts, christmas gifts, birthday gifts and on many other special occasions.

## THE POETRY OF MARY SOUTHERS

In 1944 Mary sent Thanksgiving Papers to the following people: Lula Anderson, Ms.. Gray, Ms. Reed, Miss Thomas, desk clerk,, social services clinic, clerk at window, undertaker, elevator girl, and Officer James Moore. These poems were written on all kinds of tablets and on all types of writing pads; Blue Tag, Hi-Up Writing Tablet, Universal Writing Tablet, The Worthmore Tablet, Penstar Quality Writing Tablet, The Double Q Composition Book, Louisville School Theme Tablet No. 4, and Louisville School Theme Tablet No. 5. Many of the poems were written on the back of anything Mary could find to write on. "As I Look Back Over the Hill" is written on the back of A Republican Party election letter signed by John S. Cooper and Thruston B. Morton, The poem, "He Knows All About Us" is written on the back of a 1947 United Furniture Company Christmas flyer. Other poems were written on the back of grading-progress sheets for some elementary and high school, and on the back of St. Martin Catholic Church stationary.

We were often told that our great-grandmother was a very religious and godly woman, and was blessed by the Almighty with the gift of writing. How else do you explain such writing ability with only a middle or high school education? Her only known occupation was as a housekeeper. We do not know when Mary started writing but know that "Happy at Last" was checked off as her "first poem".

This book of almost 200 poems has been divided into two books with fourteen (14) chapters for easier reading. In our attempts to remain true to the exact letters and words written by Mary Southers, changes have been made only when the words were not clear, since the original writings are now fading and sometimes difficult to discern. Bible verses have been added on a couple of pages to keep the readers interest, and as Mary says, "to point someone higher to God."

May poetry lovers and every reader throughout the world be blessed and enriched by the religious poetry and inspirational writings of Mary Southers. God blessed her with a special gift. And the truth is that no matter what gift God blesses one with, he gives you his grace so you can use that gift for his glory and honor. Mary Southers was blessed with such a gift, and our great grandmother certainly knew *how to write a line!*

*by Charles C. Hagan Jr.*

*IF I COULD ONLY WRITE A LINE*

## IF I COULD ONLY WRITE A LINE

If I could only write a line
As prophets did in olden times
A burning message of God's love
Who sent his dear Son from above
To suffer death upon the cross
And counted it as gain, not loss.

Oh, if I could only aspire
To make the reader's thoughts rise
If I could point some higher one to God
Who along the wicked way has trod
I really think I'd be content
That is what I think she meant.

He said that we should bear much fruit
So let us then in Him take root
For without roots we cannot grow
I want my life for Him to show
I only want to shine for Him
And may my glory be but dim.

I only want to say and do
The things that he would wish me to
If I can only live this way
I know I'll praise Him day by day.

*by Mary Southers*

# CHAPTER ONE

# PRAISE GOD

### WORSHIP

God speaks and I listen in wonder
He talks in the whispering leaves
In the flowers that bloom by the way side
And the drip of the rain from the eaves
The skylark is singing his praises
All nature bends low to his will
Like a prayer comes the silence of twilight
When the sun has dipped over the hill.

And they stood up in their place,
and read in the book of the law
of the LORD their God one fourth part of the day;
and another fourth part they confessed,
and worshipped the LORD their God.
**Nehemiah 9:3**

*IF I COULD ONLY WRITE A LINE*

## YOUR GIFT

Did you know you could make a crown of pearls?
One with splendor untold
A beautiful crown to give your king
Outlined with sparkling gold.

And how do you make such a crown you ask
And where are the pearls and gold?
And who is the king whose head you will crown
And how is its beauty told?

The crown that I mean is the crown for Christ
Which is fashioned every day
And each little pearl is obtained with love
Of the cross that comes our way.

The gold is the daily service you give
Making the beautiful frame
And so the splendid crown will be fashioned
When one day he'll call your name!


And when they were come into the house,
they saw the young child with Mary his mother,
and fell down, and worshipped him:
and when they had opened their treasures
they presented unto him **gifts**; gold, and frankincense and myrrh.

**Matthew 2:11**

## EMINENCE

If as at eventide we kneel
In solitude to pray
We'd thank God for the lovely things
He'd sent to us that day.

We'd lose all cognizance of fear
There'd be no aching smarts
Of bitterness because of all
The love within our hearts.

Then whence once more we'd rise to greet
A new day dawning clear
We'd need no labored struggling thought
To bring his presence near.

Nor would we seek to pierce the distant
Skyly structure dense
In search of Him for in our hearts
We'd hold his Eminence!


The mighty God, even the LORD, hath spoken
and called the earth from the rising of the sun
unto the going down thereof.
Out of Zion, the perfection of beauty, God hath shined.

**Psalms 50:1-2**

## THE ELEVATION

At the tinkle of the bell
When we pause to kneel and tell
Of our need for help and grace
Behold, he greets us face to face.

Precious moments these be sure
Sacred to the rich and poor
Sinners to there find the friend
Whoever seeks them to the end.

Look then to Him on high above
With grateful heart and fervent love
Dispel all thought of greed and hate
Remember always eternal fate.

Breathe a prayer for heavenly light
And protection in the fight
Make your answer to his call
My Lord, My God, My King, My All!

## WHAT SHALL I OFFER THEE?

What shall I give O Lord to thee
And to thy church, thy spotless bride
What portion of my means shall be
   My offering to the crucified?

O blessed Savior when I see
In vision cross-crowned Calvary
What can I give-what offer make
As fitting gift, for thy dear sake?

What rather Lord can I withhold
From thee who gave all to me
What service hard-what treasured gold
   Upon thine altar offer free?

Oh Savior dear, no gift of mine
Could ever be compared with thine
What alms or labor can I give
Like dying love, which bade me live?

What shall I bring, Oh sacred heart
Which beats for sinners-love divine
Let me not feebly offer part
Nay let my life be wholly thine?

Thus, blest redeemer at Thy call
Let me with gladness offer all
In Thy dear service wide and free
To give and give, unselfishly!

*IF I COULD ONLY WRITE A LINE*

## OH HAIL TO THE KING!

Oh hail to the King of Calvary
Who bled and died to set us free
That our lives should be consecrated unto Him
Who gave his only begotten son to bring us back to Him.

Let us sing and give praise unto our King
Who paid such a price for this world of sin
So let us lift our voices and forever sing
Oh hail to our Savior, Lord, and King

All sadness and sorrow will pass away
If we'll just be still and let Him have his way
He'll lift the burden then we can sing
Oh hail to our Savior, Lord, and King.

There's no King on earth such peace can bring
As did Jesus Christ, our Savior and King
Then with joyful hearts let us sing
Oh hail to our Savior, Lord, and King.

Though many trials and sorrow may cloud our way
But when we think of the power and mercy of God
Then we can lift up our voice and sing
Oh Hail, to our Savior, Lord and King!

written  August 7, 1949

## ASPIRATION

Dear little Babe of Bethlehem
Oh mighty king of kings
Enthroned upon a manger bed
While heavenly choirs sing.

Teach me, sweet little child divine
To walk thy little way
To know thee, love thee more and more
And serve thee day by day.

Oh smile this day upon me
Come dwell within my soul
And lead me by thy light divine
To my eternal goal!

*IF I COULD ONLY WRITE A LINE*

## TO CLOSE THE HOUSE OF GOD

Oh how could you close the house of God
When he has promised to meet us there
To come and learn of his blessed word
And the promise of his loving care.

What about lost souls going astray
Where else shall they be set free
When the doors of Gods house are closed
And no lights that they may see.

It was said, it was good when they said
"Let us go into the house of the Lord"
That we may give Him the glory and the praise
Though when we close the house of God, many souls turned away.

Who knows when a sinner may repent
And come seeking for someone to pray
To the house of God where he's promised to meet us
And the doors are locked to be turned away!


written July 7, 1949

## ONE MORNING AFTER CHURCH

There in the bright Autumn sunshine
An old couple stood after church,
They turned with a word of greeting
As I was about to pass.

And they said in their simple friendly way
How they read all my things with delight
"It must be wonderful, they said
Poems like those to write".

And I looked at that old couple standing there
In the Autumn of their days
Thoughts of the family they'd reared and trained.
Though not always sunny days.

And I mussed, Yes, I may have written
Some verse that has ground its way home
But I only wrote them while you dear old folks
By your whole lives, you've lived a poem.

*IF I COULD ONLY WRITE A LINE*

## THE BELLS ON SUNDAY MORNING

I like to hear the church bells
Ring out on Sunday morn
They bring back memories of happy days
In the town where I was born.

I used to hear the church bells ring
When I was a little lad
And my mother would say, "now get up son"
And so would my dear old dad.

And on those Sunday morns
To church I'd walk two miles
But the country way was rendered gay
By neighborly friendly smiles.

At eventide those bells still ring
In the town where I was born
But the city's tumult shuts them out
And leaves me quite forlorn.

## THE GOOD OLD-FASHIONED WAY

I love to hear the songs of Zion sung
And I love to hear God's children pray
You can feel the spirit burning in your souls
When they worship in the good old-fashioned way.

There are so many souls that are not saved
And so many souls are gone astray
All because they do not worship God
In the good old-fashioned way.

There are songs sung in harvest times today
That do not twitch the sinners soul
May God in his mercy bring us back, I pray
In the good old-fashioned way.

When Dad and Mother and many servants of God
Would bow down on their knees to God and pray
Sinners would tremble and cry for mercy
For they prayed to God in the good old-fashioned way.

written December 31, 1945

***IF I COULD ONLY WRITE A LINE***

## O, WE OF LITTLE FAITH

There are those who in these trying times
Wonder where God can be
That such terrors are permitted
Abroad on land and sea.

In the mind of many dreary doubts arise
As to ultimate destiny
And I think of what Christ told the fishermen
At the shores of Galilee.

"Save us O Lord or we perish", they cried
Adrift on a storm tossed sea
Twas then Christ addressed that message
To them and to you and to me.

"Am I not with you always
Dispelling all perils wrath"
That faith still holds today
If we trust and obey.

# CHAPTER TWO

# CHRIST OUR LORD

## COME AND FOLLOW ME

I see Him walking
In the day's blue coolness to Galilee
His footsteps making pathways
Through the cornfields golden sea.

I see Him in the woodlands
Where silver brooks flow
And I see Him by the seashore
In the twilights ruby glow.

I see Him in the city
Where he lays a tender hand
On the flesh of the wounded
In a gray and stony land.

But no matter where I see Him
Always I seem to see
His lips the same sweet words caressing
Come and follow me.

***IF I COULD ONLY WRITE A LINE***

## THE FATHER'S LOVE

There are marvelous words in the Bible,
That show with what hunger of the heart
The Father is looking for His children
From self and it's greed set apart.

Who love Him because He is lovely,
Who serve Him because He is ours
Who praise His dear name with joy and acclaim
Till earth wakes anew to Hs power.

There are beautiful words in the Bible
How his bright lillies he doth feed,
How his spirit desires to love us,
Because in his hunger he needs.

And He's writing a book of Remembrance,
To last while the ages grow dim
A book of love deeds, because he has need
Of what's done in remembrance of Him.

## THE TRUTH SHALL LIVE

A lie will fail, but the truth shall live forever
It was proved nineteen hundred years ago
On Calvary's hill, on the cross, where Jesus died
For the poor lost sinners here below.

When they took Him to Pilate to be tried
He told them that his kingdom was not of this world
But they did not believe Him and said, "away with Him"
But he said that the truth shall rise again.

And after they had crucified Him
And had laid Him in the tomb
He arose on the third day, and said
"Whosoever will let Him come unto me and be saved.

For I am he that was dead
But lo, I am alive
For evermore to give
To everyone that believeth".


writtten September 18, 1946

***IF I COULD ONLY WRITE A LINE***

## HIS EYES

Oh I have seen the weary eyes
The eyes of hurt and pain
And I have seen the weeping eyes
The eyes that weep in vain.

And I have gazed at fearful eyes
Of sick bewildered brains
Yes, I have watched the empty eyes
That look but do not see.

And I have had the feeble eyes
Of age look sad at me
But oh, those eyes, those dying eyes
That gaze from Calvary.

The LORD your God who goes before you
will himself fight for you,
just as he did for you in Egypt before your eyes,

**Deuteronomy 1:30**

***THE POETRY OF MARY SOUTHERS***

## HE KNOWS ALL ABOUT US

I'm so glad that God knows all about us
As we travel from day to day
For if he didn't lead and guide us
We would surely lose our way.

For we know that without Him to guide us
That we would soon go astray
But with his tender mercy
He leads us all the way.

When we're pressed down with trouble and sorrow
And we do not know what to do
He speaks to us with tender mercy and says
Lo, I'll be with you all the way.

Oh, I am so thankful that he knows all about me
And I am so thankful that I know Him too
And if I can just serve you more and more each day
Oh Lord how I do thank you!


started September 19, 1947

*IF I COULD ONLY WRITE A LINE*

## AS UNTO HIM

Whatever you think, both in joy and in woe
Think nothing you would not like Jesus to know
Whatever you say, in a whisper or cheer
Say nothing you would not like Jesus to hear.

Whatever you read, though the page may allure
Read nothing unless you are perfectly sure
Consternation would not be seen in your look,
If God should say solemnly, show me that book.

Whatever you write, in haste or in heed,
Write nothing you would not want Jesus to read,
Whatever you sing in the midst of your glees
Sing nothing God's listening ear would displease.

Wherever you go,
Never go where you'd fear
God's question being asked you
What doest thou here?

*THE POETRY OF MARY SOUTHERS*

## THE WOUNDED SAVIOR

It was on that cold and dark night
That Christ our Lord did lay
Going through such suffering and pain
That we poor mortals might be saved.

Oh what a debt that we owe to Him
Then we should strive to serve Him each day
And no matter how hard that we may strive
To Him, we will never repay.

Oh how tired and worn he must have been
When they drug Him around all night in the judgment hall
Then carrying that heavy cross up Calvary's hill
To finish the work that he came to do for us all.

Oh what beauty there is in the Cross
Our hope, our life, our all
And He is always listening for his children
Whenever we may call.

started December 9, 1947
finished January 9, 1948

*IF I COULD ONLY WRITE A LINE*

## IN BETHLEHEM

The greatest man that was ever born
Was born in Bethlehem
Who was fought every step of the way to the cross
But he conquered in the end.

As it is today, men's eyes were blind
And they put their trust in men
They would not believe the Son of God
But victory was his in the end.

Men put their trust in material things
But he put his trust in his father God
And fought as no other man has fought
And he won the battle in the end.

So it is with his children today
When Satan fights us long and hard
The great Captain that was born in Bethlehem
Will fight our battle and we'll win in the end.

Although the enemy may fight you hard
If thou will only contend
He'll never leave or forsake you
But he'll be with you until the end.

written July 25, 1947 a.m.

## TEMPTATION CONQUERED

One night Christ and I walked up a hill
All the world was dark and still
I was weak, I staggered that night
But I held Christ's hand, I held it tight.

Christ watched me with understanding eye
As I fought to stifle my bitter cries
My enemy watched with a smirking grin
As he struck at me again and again.

I pressed close, closer to Christ's side
Behold my enemy's smile had died
Without faltering, Christ and I walked on
I was no longer weak, I was strong.

I held Christ's hand
All was well
The devil head bowed
Returned to hell!

***IF I COULD ONLY WRITE A LINE***

## JESUS IS THERE

The world has grown so wicked
That it seems there is no peace anywhere
But through all of its sin and sorrow
I know that Jesus is there.

When it seems like that all the world is against you
And you know not which way to go
Just always remember that you're not alone
For Jesus is there I know.

Oh, it's so wonderful to know
That there is always a friend to whom you can go
For when the burden seems too heavy to bear
I know that Jesus is there to share.

When the trials of this wicked world of sin
Have bruised our heart until its sore
And our very souls bleed within
Jesus is there to help us I know.

If we will only let Him have our sorrows
And would only look to Him more
Every thing will be all right in time
Jesus is there to help us I know.

written January 21, 1945

## CARRYING CHRIST

Into the hillside country Mary went
Carrying Christ, and all along the way
The Christ she carried generously bestowed
His grace on those she met.

To tell she carried Christ, she was content
To hide his love for her
But about her glowed such joy that
Into stony hearts love flowed.

And even to the unborn John
Christ's grace was sent
Christ in his sacrament of love each day
Dwells in my soul a little space and then.

I walk life's crowded highway jostling men
Who seldom think of God
To these I pray that I may carry Christ
For it may be some would not know of Him except for me.

## CROWNS

When you give up some cherished earthly pleasure
And work for the Lord instead
Because of your love for Him, and His dear cause
You are casting your crown before Him
For the Christ who for you bled.

You do not have to wait till you get to heaven
You can glorify Him here
Hold out your hand to your fellow man
And help the afflicted one to stand
And dry his falling tear.

It may be only an earthly crown of joy or pride
We are casting down at His feet
But he knows it's the best we can do down here
And he counts it a gift complete!

And round about the throne were four and twenty seats:
and upon the seats I saw four and twenty elders sitting
clothed in white raiment; and they had on their heads crowns of gold.

**Revelations 4:4**

## OUR GUIDE

The Bible is our only guide
In this dark world of sin and woe
And if we will only follow it
It will lead us home I know.

We may have sorrow and disappointments
And feel friendless and all alone
But just look up to Jesus, our Savior
And he will surely lead us home.

When the world is dark and gloomy
And it seems that there is no light
If we would only look up to our Savior
Then all things would be bright.

For he said, I am the light and the way
Without me no light can be
And if we will only follow Him
He'll lead us on to victory.

For he is able to do all things you see
There is nothing that he can't do
For when man has gone to his limits
Then it's God's opportunity to do.

Dear Lord, you have done so much for me
For which I shall forever give you the praise
And please, Dear God, forever hold my hand
And lead me home to thee.

written October 8, 1944

*IF I COULD ONLY WRITE A LINE*

## GOD OUR KING

Oh how wonderful it is too sing
The praises of Jesus our prince and King
Who gave His life that we might live
And to Him our praises we must give.

How wonderful it was on that first Christmas morn
When in the Manger our king was born
And all over the world the angels sing
Hosanna to our Prince and King.

Oh what a privilege that we have
That we too can lift up our voice and sing
As the wise men did on Christmas day
Glory to God, and to our Prince and King.

Though we may go through much sorrow
And bear much suffering and pain
But through it all thank God we can sing
Glory to God, Our Savior, and King!

finished November 26, 1947

## HE HAS RISEN

When they had crucified Jesus on the cross
To Mary, his mother, and his disciples it was a great loss.

But to their loss it was gain
For as he had told them on the third day I shall rise again.

And on the third day just as he said
Our Lord, and Master, did rise from the grave.

That whosoever will might be saved
For he knows the power over death and the grave.

Then let us thank God for this Easter day
For His son, who has risen to lead the way.

From this earth's sorrow to heavens joy
Where we can be with Him and his love enjoy.

*IF I COULD ONLY WRITE A LINE*

## I'M ALWAYS NEAR

Come down to earth, O Lord
And walk the way with me
For I am sorely tempted
And need to learn of Thee.

Go with me through the valley
Where I must walk and weep
Come nearer and give thy solace
When I lie down to sleep.

Go with me over the mountains
Where the road is rough and steep
And cheer me by Thy presence
When my weary eyelids weep.

Come thou when all is darkness
Shed sunshine along my way
Be thou so very near me
I can hear what thou has to say.

Give me strength along my journey
When my heart doth seem to fail
Be my armor and breastplate
When Satan's hosts assail.

## FOR ME HE CAME

For me he left his home on high
For me to earth he came to die
For me in a manger lay
For me to Egypt fled away.

For me he dwelt with fishermen
For me he dwelt in cave and glen
For me abuse he meekly bore
For me a crown of thorns he wore.

For me he loved Gethsemane
For me he hung upon a tree
For me his final feast was made
For me by Judas was betrayed.

For me by Peter was denied
For me by Pilate crucified
For me his precious blood was shed
For me he slept among the dead.

For me he rose with might at last
For me above the skies he passed
For me he came at God's command
For me he sits at his right hand.

*IF I COULD ONLY WRITE A LINE*

## I KNOW JESUS AND HE KNOWS ME

I'm so glad that Jesus set me free
When He died upon the cross on Calvary
That I might let my light shine so others may see
That I know Jesus and he knows me.

Though sometimes it seems there's nothing but dark clouds
Yet down in my heart I want to holler loud
That through the darkness and no matter how dark it may be
That I can say that I know Jesus and he knows me.

The lightning may flash and the thunder may roll
But deep down in my heart he speaks to my weary soul
And says don't give up but live that others may see
That I know Jesus and he knows me.

And some day the dark clouds will roll away
Then Jesus, Himself, my reward will pay
If I'll just live so that other's may see
That I know Jesus and he knows me.

For we were bought with a price on Calvary's hill
And the promise that he made then, he now makes still
If you own me, then I'll own thee and the world shall know
That I know Jesus and he knows me.

## THE POETRY OF MARY SOUTHERS

## OVER TWO THOUSAND YEARS AGO

Over two thousand, years ago
Christ our Lord was born
To bring man back to God
Who was lost and forlorn.

Then with what love that we should have
For Him who loved us so
To leave his home of peace and love
And come down in this wicked world below.

He who bore our burdens all along the way
Until that day should come
That He with His life must pay
For the lost and guilty one.

And when that cruel day did come
He did not for forsake us then
But He paid the debt for you and I
That peace on earth should rule among men.

Now since he gave his life for us
That through Him we might live
Then we should strive with all our heart
To Him all our service to give.

Then let us shout and praise his name
And praise our dear God the same
That out of his love his only begotten Son he gave
That our lost souls might be saved.

written December 23, 1944

*IF I COULD ONLY WRITE A LINE*

## THE BABE OF BETHLEHEM

Christ the name that will never die
That was born on Christmas day
The child that was born in Bethlehem
In a manager among the new morn hay.

No joy has ever been in this world
As it was on the morning of that day
When he, was laid in the manger so sweet
On the morning of that first Christmas day.

Oh if that love was in this world today
And the peace that with Him came
It would be a lovely world to live in
Praising his holy name.

Oh Lord bring back that peace, and love
That came down from above that day
That we may love each other true
With that love that can't be taken away.

He who conquered death and the grave
That can kill dead and then make alive
Who arose, with all power in heaven and in earth
Now sits in heaven by his Father's side.

Oh hallelujah, praise his name
Oh help us to praise his holy name
Let's sing the songs that the angels sing
To Christ, the newborn Savior, and King.

Peace on earth, good will toward men!

written October 28, 1944

## HE WHO SEES THE SPARROW

He who sees the sparrow fall
And the hair that falls from your head
Also sees the works of the enemy
On his way with his evil to spread.

And when he with his evil hits its blow
He thinks in his heart that it's all over
But he who sees the sparrow fall
Will surely hear you when you call.

For he is always listening when we call
When the enemy strikes great or small
For he has protecting love for all
He who sees the sparrow fall.

Oh I'm so glad that he cares for me
And that under his wing he shelters me
So if I stay with Him no harm can be
For he'll forever watch over me.

Though it may thunder and it may rage
But my God is there and he will save
For he who sees the sparrow fall
Keeps tender watch over us all.

written Sept. 25, 1944

*IF I COULD ONLY WRITE A LINE*

## CHRIST IS VICTORY!

All over the world men are crying
We want to be free
But still they won't turn and look to God
For Christ is Victory.

If all men would keep Gods commandments
Then all men would be free
For God said, "this is my beloved Son, hear ye Him"
For Christ is victory.

For over nineteen hundred years ago
Christ died upon the tree
Deliver us from the enemy
For Christ is Victory.

There will never be peace in this world
Or freedom or real victory will ever be,
Until men's hearts are clean and full of love
For Christ is Victory.

There has been many a man whose life was lost,
Who tried fighting to bring victory
But when Jesus died upon the cross
He said, "I am Victory."

written November 6, 1945

***THE POETRY OF MARY SOUTHERS***

## THAT'S THE WAY THEY DID OUR SAVIOR

We find some friends that say I love you
On me you can depend
And when the time comes you need them they forsake you in the end
But that's the way they did our savior.

They will tell you that they love you
And when you see them you get a frown instead of a smile
And offtimes they will scorn you too
But that's the way they did our savior.

Sometimes they smile to your face
And again they will stab you behind your back
But thank God that we have learned in his word
That that's the way they did our savior.

They will say that they are trying to help you
And they are tearing you down all the time
But they did not deceive my savior
For he knew them all the time.

But as our Savior overcame
As a servant of his will, we will too
For he said I've overcome the world
If you put your trust in me, so shall you.

written June 3, 1947 a.m.

*IF I COULD ONLY WRITE A LINE*

## CHAPTER THREE

## SOLDIERS AND ARMIES

### NO UNKNOWN SOLDIER

Tonight on a lonely snow swept street
A soldier and I happened to meet
I stood to one side as he struggled by
Battling the drifts almost elbow high.

His suitcase was heavy that much I could see
But I looked at him and he grinned at me
So I said, "Hello", for why shouldn't I greet
A soldier I met on a storm swept street.

I didn't know him, he didn't know me
But that needn't matter for all I could see
So I talked and we talked and he seemed right glad
And told of the furlough home he just had.

Then we dropped in a place for a bite to eat
He seemed so pleased with the little treat
Then he went his way and I went mine
I can still see those honest young grateful eyes shine.

## THE UNPAYABLE DEBT

What have I given
And what have I done
That you fought for me
With heart and with gun.

And what can I do
To pay for your deed
To erase your burden
And follow your creed.

Yes, what can I do
For you soldier brave
As long as I live
For the lives you gave.

For all you have done
I can give you tears
And promise to pray
All the rest of my years.

## OUR BOYS PRAYER

O God, I love and trust in Thee
Please take me safe across the sea
And when I land please take my hand
And guide me where I have to stand.

I'll pray to you both night and day
And let me here not long to stay
And when my duty and work is done
And Victory over the world is won.

Please bring me back
To the home I love
All thanks to you
Dear God above.

<u>Luke 11:1 It happened that while Jesus was praying in a certain</u> ... certain place. After he had finished, one of his disciples said to him, "Lord, **teach us** to **pray**, as John taught his disciples." ...

***IF I COULD ONLY WRITE A LINE***

## THE WEIGHT OF ALL FLESH

Johnny wrote in his first letter
The army makes my health much better

Just the other day I found
My weight increased by sixty-pounds.

Fifteen pounds of clothes and trifle
And forty-five of pack and rifle.

## WE WITHOUT SONS

I've never had a son
Still when those boys marched by today
Their fine young lives but just begun.

I sensed a kinship with each one
And I felt as I'd never felt before
We are brothers all and forever more.

I've never had a son
Yet when those boys marched by today
Barely done with their years of play

I knew what those mothers were going through.
As they quietly stood there, the fathers too.
And I said to myself as I turned away

Even we without sons
Can watch and pray.

## AN UNKNOWN SOLDIER IN TIMES LIKE THESE

An unknown soldier in times like these
Should be an unheard of thing, so please
Remember just this, they're fighting your fight
So to hold them as strangers would hardly be right.

They've given up home and friends and laughter
To do their bit for the ones to come after
So the next lonely soldier you happen to meet
Walk a piece with him along friendship street.

## GOD'S ARMY

I shall march on and on men
Despite your purging and your sin
I shall march on and on Oh world
Despite the accusations hurled.

Still my children by the score
They will never fear death's dark door
Open it men throw it wide
They will march through side by side.

Until the end of time shall be
Persecutions cannot destroy me
Though you release the furies of hell
I will march on and never fail.

I will be after you have turned to dust
I will outlive man's greed and lust
I am the church militant, my captain divine
Leads my army until the end of time.

*IF I COULD ONLY WRITE A LINE*

## SOLDIERS OF CHRIST

Soldiers of Christ we have pledged to be
With Him we're certain of victory
Eager we wait what his will may send
Whatever he commands our hearts and hands are his to the end.

Though dangers assail shall we hide or run
Though we falter and quail is the cause undone?
Though we fall, we will rise, and despite the pain
With effort and strain, we'll struggle again till victory is won.

Childhood's play is o'er
And now the day of sterner duty is beginning
Soon to faithful friends and alma mater
We must bid a fond farewell.

Golden dreams before us gleam
And show us a prize worthy of our winning
And love will lend us courage glowing
As on we're going towards that bright goal
To which our way must never end.

# THE POETRY OF MARY SOUTHERS

## THERE'S ANOTHER ARMY

Uncle Sam and the allies
Have the greatest army they say
But there's another army
That excels all armies today.

This army that I'm talking about
Is the army of Christ you see
For he with his blood called soldiers
Over nineteen hundred years ago on Calvary.

For when he gave his life that day
To set the poor sinner free
He said, "take up thy cross daily
And come and follow me".

For he's a Captain who's never lost a battle
Who knows when to attack the enemy you see
And without a doubt, we'll win the battle
If Jesus only our Captain will be.

For he's a light that sitteth on a hill
That all the world may see
For with Him we can do all things
And without Him nothing can be.

For he conquered death hell and the grave
Without any weapons you see
For he's the son of our Creator God
Who has all power to set us free.

So fight on brave soldiers, fight on to the end
Until the victory is won and then
We can sing the song that the angels sang
Peace on earth goodwill to men.

written June 11, 1944

*IF I COULD ONLY WRITE A LINE*

# CHAPTER FOUR

# PRAYERS

### GOD WE THANK YOU

O God, for another day
For another morning
For another hour
For another minute
For another chance
To live and serve Thee
I am grateful.

Do thou this day free me
From fear of the future
From anxiety of tomorrow
From bitterness towards anyone
From cowardice in danger
From laziness in face of work
From failure before opportunity
From weakness when thy power is at work.

But fill me with
Love that knows no barriers
Courage that cannot be shaken,
Faith strong enough for the darkness
Strength sufficient for my task
Loyalty to Thy Kingdoms goal
Wisdom to meet life's complexities.

As thou will in Christ's name, I pray.
AMEN!

## THE TRAVELER'S MORNING OFFERING

I travel with ever changing goal
But over land, Dear Lord or over sea
In wider panoramas of the soul
Thy constant feet are traveling with me.


## COMFORT

Some things we think are gold
Prove only brass
Life and the world still teach us
As they pass.

But oh the peace that comes into a soul
Who comes to say
Unto a thinking heart
From day to day.

What matters if time brings
But shadows gray
If you can pray!

***THE POETRY OF MARY SOUTHERS***

## OUR MASTER IS THERE

Don't despair my dear one
Just place yourself in your Savior's care
For he's the head physician
And I know that he is there.

Sometimes it seems that all hope is gone
And it causes us great distress
But that is his way of showing us
That our heavenly father knows best.

His divine spirit leads the doctor's
And teaches them just what to do
So just have faith in Jesus and the doctor
And by his power you will surely pull through.

written July 4, 1946

Jeremiah asked this famous rhetorical question Jer. 8:22.

"Is there no balm in Gilead?
Is there no physician there?
Why then has not the health of the daughter of my people been restored?"

## **LEARNING CHRIST**

Teach me, my Lord, to be sweet and gentle
In all the events of life
In disappointments
In the thoughtlessness of others
In the insincerity of others I trusted
In the unfaithfulness of those on whom I relied.

Let me put myself aside
To think of the happiness of others
To hide my little pains and heartaches
So that I may be the only one to suffer from them.

Teach me to profit by the suffering
That comes across my path.
Let me so use it that it mellows me
That it may make me patient, not irritable
That it may make me broad in my forgiveness
Not narrow, haughty, and overbearing.

May no one be less good for having
Been a fellow traveler in our journey towards Eternal life
As I go my rounds from one distraction to another
Let me whisper from time to time
A word of love to thee.

May my life be lived in the supernatural
Full of power for good and strong
In its purpose of sanctity.

*THE POETRY OF MARY SOUTHERS*

## MY PRAYER FOR THEE

Figure on the cross above
Fill my heart with purest love
Hand so precious torn by nail
Help me rise whenever I fail.

Head now bowing
Crowned with thorns,
Leave me not alone forlorn.

Heart of Jesus pierced by spear
Guide my steps, dispel my fear
Figure on the cross above
Fill my heart with purest love.




Now before the feast of the passover,
when Jesus knew that his hour was come
that he should depart out of this world unto the Father,
having loved his own which were in the world,
he loved them unto the end.

**John 13:1**

*IF I COULD ONLY WRITE A LINE*

## THEY BELONG TO THEE

Oh, my Jesus, bless my children
How I plead that they may be
Children of Thy love, my Jesus
May they live and die for Thee.

I thank thee for thy gift so dear
With thy grace I fain would be
Mother of a thousand children
Just to give them all to thee.

Take their love, I do not want it
Take their hearts, they are Thine own
Yeah, my greatest joy to find that
They belong to Thee alone.

Disciples, and Prophets -ah! could it be?
Not as I will, but as Thou wilt.
Take them, they belong to Thee!
Oh, dear Jesus, grant it please.

*THE POETRY OF MARY SOUTHERS*

## BLESS THOU ME OH MOTHER

Bless thou me O Mother!
Bless thou me thy child
Thee I call no other
Virgin Mother mild.

Bless my thoughts and actions
All the livelong day
Keep me from distractions
When I try to pray.

Bless thou, too O Mother!
All the friends I love
Father, Mother, Brother
And the ones above.

Lay thy hands in blessing
On the whole wide earth
Tenderly caressing
The hand that gives one birth.

Bless thou me, O Mother!
When our work is done
And the angels whisper
It is time to come.

May we be awakened
By thy lily hand
And by thee be taken
To the Promised Land.

***IF I COULD ONLY WRITE A LINE***

## LO, THESE MANY YEARS

I thank you dear God for your guidance
Though many sorrows, grief, and tears
For I know that you have been with me
Lo these many years.

There has been many a time that my heart was heavy
And my cheek's wet with briny tears
But you have been my only comfort
Lo these many years.

For you were a man of sorrow
And you also were acquainted with grief
And I thank you dear Lord for keeping me
Lo these many years.

The way had been so dark and gloomy
That I could hardly see my way
But I thank you dear Lord for the peace that you
Have brought to my heart, lo these many years.

Dear God, please help me to grow strong
Please move away all doubts and fears
For I know that you have been with all generations
For lo these many years.

written September 26, 1945 @ 1:00 a.m.
for Thanksgiving

## JESUS HELP ME

Oh Jesus, help me I plead
To be satisfied walking with Thee
For when all other help is gone
You promised not to leave me alone.

He who sits upon His throne
Has promised to take care of his own
Who sees and pities every groan
Will not leave his children alone.

I thank you, dear God above
For your kind and tender Love
Please help me I beg of Thee
To forever stay close to Thee.

Oh help me dear God to be still
And strive to do thy Holy will
Please dear Jesus forever be with me.
And lead me on to victory.

And whenever my heart is sad
Please help me to rejoice and be glad
For that's what you told us to do
For they did the same unto you.

*IF I COULD ONLY WRITE A LINE*

# CHAPTER FIVE

# LIFE'S PRACTICAL LESSONS

## WIT ENDS CORNER

Are you standing at wits end corner
Christian with troubled brow?
Are you thinking of what is before you
And all you are bearing now?

Has all the world seemed against you,
And you in the battle alone?
Remember at wits end corner
Is just where God's power is shown!

Are you standing at wits end corner?
Then you're just in the very spot
To learn the wondrous resources
Of Him who faileth not.

No doubt to a brighter pathway
Your footsteps will soon be moved,
But only at wits end corner
Is the God who is able proved.

*IF I COULD ONLY WRITE A LINE*

## GOD DOES NOT FORGET

The world will strip your failings
And hide the good you do
And with its sharpest thorns
The ways you walk bestrew.

You'll toil for men - they'll curse you
It was thus and thus tis yet
And thus it will be forever
But God will not forget.

The hours of silent grieving
For someone loved and lost
The hours of self denial
Was hard to count the cost.

The falling soul uplifted
The sorrows bravely met
All on earth forgotten
But God does not forget.

His eye is ever seeking
The wee things done for Him
And that shall light the shadows
Where death waits stern and grim.

So lift your burden gladly
Nor falter, fear, or fret
For heaven is in the distance
And God does not forget.

***THE POETRY OF MARY SOUTHERS***

## A CLEAN HEART

Now that nineteen hundred and forty-six
Appears upon the scene
I am thankful I begin it
With a heart that is clean.

Not clean through any merit
Or goodness of my own
But made so through the blood
Of the all sufficient one.

## SCIENCE OF FORGETTING

O birds that sing with thoughtful psalm
Rebuking human fretting
Teach us your secret of content
Your science of forgetting.

For every life must have its ills
You too have hours of sorrow
Teach us like you to lay them by
And sing again tomorrow.

For gems of darkness yet may lie
Within a golden setting
And he is wise who understands
The science of forgetting.

*IF I COULD ONLY WRITE A LINE*

## HEART TENANTS

The wills, the wants, and the cants
Have rooms in the house of life
The wills are peaceable folk
But the wants and the cants mark strife.

The wills accomplish much good
The wants oppose and defy
The cant's see failure ahead
And never will say, I'll try.

These last, two tenants should go
So ask them now to depart
Then seek, more folk like the wills
To rent the rooms in your heart.

Blessed are the peacemakers:
for they shall be called the children of God.

**Matthew 5:9**

*THE POETRY OF MARY SOUTHERS*

## KINDNESS

Kindness is a magic key
Easy to use, but hard to see
It opens most any portal wide
Though other keys may have been tried.

A heart that's locked is sad to see
It lies imprisoned never free
It waits and yearns for a friend to give
One look, one word, to make it live.

Many a man may be condemned
And ridiculed by foe and friend
"He's bad" they say "he's bad clear through"
He isn't as good as I or you.

That's not true, it's most unfair
Let's try kindness if we dare
And see what wonders we can do
For one they say is "bad clear through"!

## SEDATIVE

Speak your piece
Do your best
Let your faith
Work out the rest.

If your conscience says
You've done what's right
You won't need a pill
To sleep at night.


## TWO WAY RULE

Having a friend is a wonderful thing
A friend who is loyal and true
But then have you ever stopped to think
That being a friend's nice too.

To have a friend is a comforting thing
But that is just solace for you
So remember the other fellow needs
Try being a good friend too.

*THE POETRY OF MARY SOUTHERS*

## BREAD UPON THE WATERS

I never keep books on favors
Or figures under my hats
Now, I have done such for so and so
So I ought to get this for that.

Whenever I do a favor
I'm glad that I have it to spare
I like the person I'm doing it for
And the matter's forgotten right there.

No, I never keep books on favors
Or wonder just when they'll repay
For bread upon the waters, I've found
Comes back in its own time and way.

Someday this kindness will come back to you!

written June 1, 1944

*IF I COULD ONLY WRITE A LINE*

## YOU'LL HAVE TO DO IT OR MAKE IT

Of all the excuses there are
By which this old world is accursed
This haven't got time is by far
The poorest, the feeblest, the worst.

A delusion it is, and a snare
If the habit is yours, you should shake it
For if you want to do what is offered to you
You'll find time to do it or make it.

## LIVE FOR SOMETHING

Live for something and lie in earnest
Though the work may humble be
By the word of men unnoticed
Known alone to God and thee.

Every act has priceless value
To the architect of fate
Tis the spirit of doing
That alone will make it great.

Live for something—God and Angels
Are they watchers in the strife?
And above the smoke and conflict
Gleams the victors crown of life.

Live for something, God has given
Freely of His stores divine
Richest gifts of earth and Heaven
If thou willest, may be thine!

## O HASTE

The things we might have done
But which we failed to do
They hunt us every one
And pass us in review.

The words we might have said
The aid we might have lent
But now the moment fled
Remains but sad lament.

The opportunity
We did not seize when ours
The prodigality
With which we spent our powers.

But now, regret is vain
And useless are our tears
They'll not bring back again
The chances of past years.

The succor merely planned
The help we failed to give
At duty's stern command
Regrets alone, now live.

Alas for deeds undone
Alas for words unsaid
God help us everyone
Redeem the years ahead!

*IF I COULD ONLY WRITE A LINE*

# CHAPTER SIX

# MOTHERHOOD

### OH! THE LOVE OF MOTHER

Exceeding the love of Jesus
There is no love on earth like mother
When all other love on earth has failed
You can depend on Jesus and mother.

Mother stands by what ever betide
Ready to give a helping hand
Through many weary days and sleepless nights
But by Jesus side she'll stand.

Jesus knew the love of his mother
As at the foot of the cross she did stand
And he sought a home for her before he died
And placed her in his beloved disciples hand.

Through all the agony and sorrow
Mother is always standing by
Dear Lord, I thank you for my mother
For on her I know I can rely.

written May 2, 1949

*IF I COULD ONLY WRITE A LINE*

## MOTHER ON CALVARY'S HILL

As my mind runs back o'er the hill of time
I think of the Virgin Mary, Jesus' mother
As I see them both traveling up Calvary's hill
To teach us the love of Mother.

While hanging on the cross
With sweat, blood, and tears flowing down his face
He said, "John behold thy mother"
For he knew that in this world there would be no other
Than the Virgin Mary, his mother.

Oh what a burden rolled from her heart
When she talked to his father God
For the sun shown brighter on that Easter morn
Covering the tracks from which he trod.

Oh how blessed is the name mother
For her love is next to the love of God
There is no love in this world like mother
For mother was sent from God.

God chose the Virgin Mary for his son's mother
And she stood by Him unto the end
And our mother's is just as faithful
For she'll stay with us, on that we can depend.

started May 11, 1947

*THE POETRY OF MARY SOUTHERS*

## MY MOTHER

Oh Lord, I have not the words to say
On this mother's day
In thankfulness to you for my Mother
On this another mothers day.

Dear Lord, please help me to love
And cherish my mother
For the love that she has shown to me
That her life may be happy and free.

May we always keep her teaching
And be humble and grateful to Thee.
May nothing ever separate us dear God,
From our dear Mother and Thee.

written Mother's Day May 5, 1945

*IF I COULD ONLY WRITE A LINE*

## DEAR MOTHER

Dear mother, oh how much I miss you today
I haven't the words to say
I miss your smiling face so much
And those sweet and tender words you used to say.

I miss those words of courage and tender love
That will always live within my heart
Until I shall meet you dear mother
In that land where we shall never more part.

Sleep on, in peace, dear mother and take your rest
From the toil and trials of this world
May the Lord help us to live as you did mother
And let His banner be unfurled.

On this mother's day, mother dear,
Every thing seems so empty without you,
But God's will has been done,
And by His grace some day we will see you again.

## TO MY SON

Dear son, it seems but yesterday
Your heart lay on my arm
My mother's love surrounded you
And kept you safe from harm.

Soon your toddling footsteps
Followed ever after me
Then you walked beside me
And we talked in comradery.

Now your stride has lengthened
You are girding for the race
Son, you must not miss the trophy
Just because I can't keep pace.

I will rest me by the wayside
Following after as I can
But my love will run beside you
Urging you to play the man.

You're the crown of my existence
Pride in you just fills my soul
You are my incarnate spirit
Pressing onward toward the goal.

*IF I COULD ONLY WRITE A LINE*

## MOTHER OF MINE

Oh, mother of mine
How I do adore you
Although you're so far away
The things that you taught me dear mother
Still lives in my heart today.

You taught me to love Jesus, my dear mother
And His commandments to obey
And to hold to His unchanging hand
That He'd lead me all the way.

Although you're not with me, mother dear
Your spirit seems to be so near
I can still hear your sweet voice, dear mother
Whispering in my ear so clear.

It gives me strength, dear mother
While along this weary road I must trod
And If I live the way that you taught me
I know it will lead me home to God.

As the dear mother of Jesus so tenderly
Kept watch over the infant Jesus long ago
So did you teach me dear mother
That Jesus would save my soul.

And I thank you so much mother dear,
For teaching me about the good old way
For I know, that if I live as you taught me
I will see you again someday.

written January 8, 1946

### *THE POETRY OF MARY SOUTHERS*

## AS GRANNY IS TODAY

Some daily count their sorrows
Some find joy and sorrow blends
Some are happy counting money
But granny counts her friends.

Some only love the old folks
Some the children small
Some the younger generation
But granny loves them all.

But listen- "the best is yet to be"
I'm sure you'll say tis true
For as she loves them everyone
They all love Granny too.

Her porch is a happy meeting place
For friends to stop awhile
And if a stranger happens in
Granny has a welcome smile.

Should my span of life reach '81
This I would daily pray
As I grow old, keep me young in heart
As Granny is today.

*IF I COULD ONLY WRITE A LINE*

## JUST TOOK A LITTLE WALK WITH THE LORD

When trials press us and the way is hard
And our only help is from God
Let's not be discouraged nor give up hope
But forever walk with the Lord.

And when it seems that we can no farther go
And the sorrow's press us until our hears are sore
We will overcome all sorrow some day I know
When we take a little walk with the Lord.

When I have shed my last tear and all is o'er
And I have gone the last mile in this life
And when my footsteps are stopped to be heard no more
Just say that I took a little walk with the Lord.

When I've walked the last mile of sorrow
And have wound up the last ball of tears
Just remember that I told you
That I just took a little walk with the Lord.

written September 18, 1946

## MOTHER HAS FALLEN ASLEEP

Mother was tired and weary
Weary with toil and pain
Put away her glasses and rocker
She will not need them again.

Into heaven's mansions she's entered
Never to worry nor weep
After long year's with life's struggles
Mother has fallen asleep.

Near other loved ones we laid her
Low in the grave to lie
God up in heaven knew best
And we will not question why.

She does not rest beneath the grasses
Though over her grave they may creep
Mother has gone to be with Jesus
She has just fallen asleep.

Rest tired feet now forever
Dear wrinkled hands are so still
Blast of the earths shall no longer
Throw o'er our loved one a chill.

Angels through heaven will guide her
Jesus will still bless and keep
Not for the world would we wake her
Mother has fallen asleep.

Beautiful rest for the weary
Well deserved rest for the true
When life's journey is ended
We shall again be with you.

*IF I COULD ONLY WRITE A LINE*

## CHAPTER SEVEN

## FRIENDSHIP

### THE FRIENDLY STREET

I always choose a friendly street
When I go out to walk
Where people smile as they pass by
And even stop to talk.

Their houses do not stand in rows
Like soldiers on parade
But they have lawns and friendly trees
That offer grateful shade.

The blinds are rolled up to the top
The windows open wide
Inviting every passer by
To take a peep inside.

Such gentle, kindly folk you see
They must be God's elite
Somehow it brings you nearer Him
Just walking down that street.

*IF I COULD ONLY WRITE A LINE*

## SOMETIMES I WONDER WHY

Sometimes I wonder why
That with some folks, life's not worthwhile
And why that love cannot abide
Instead of strife and pride.

Instead of love there is hate
And instead of peace there's strife
When it's so easy to love each other
Sometimes I wonder why.

When God is the father of us all
Yet some of us look at each other with such hate and scorn
They will not accept each other as brothers
Sometimes I wonder why.

There's but one heaven for us all
Where we must all live together some day
Yet we make life so dark living together here
Sometimes I wonder why.

When we are all bought with a price
By the blood of Jesus Christ,
Our Lord out of love
Sometimes I wonder why.

written July 4, 1946

## I HAVE A FRIEND

I have a friend, a friend who is true
I friend I can tell every sorrow to
I have a friend who stands by my side
A friend in whom all things I confide.


I have a friend, one beyond compare
Oh, world, a loyal friend is rare
I have a friend who passed the test
I have one friend, I am truly blessed.

A man that hath **friends** must shew himself friendly:
and there is a friend that sticketh closer than a brother.

**Proverbs 18:24**

*IF I COULD ONLY WRITE A LINE*

## LOVE THAT WILL NOT LET THEE GO

Oh love that will not let thee go
Help us this day to sing
The song that the angels sang
Hosanna to the new born King.

He, who left His home on high
To lay in the manger of hay
And when the shepherds saw the star
And they came to worship Him that day.

Oh blessed Lamb, Oh precious King
Help us Thy praises to sing
Forever live within our hearts
That our praises to Thee will cling.

Oh Love that will not let thee go
May we forever hold Thy hand
Until this cruel life is over
And we have reached that blessed Promised Land.

We thank you dear God
For the gift that you gave
When you gave your only begotten son
That our lost souls might be saved.

Oh glorious cross, Oh precious Lamb
All thanks and praises to Thee we sing
May we never loose the glimpse of the Cross
Until we are safely at home with Thee.

Oh, if wicked men and women everywhere
Could only realize such love
Then they would be so happy to know
That they will live with Him above.

## OVER ALL IS LOVE

Into our lives the trials come
And shadows hide the light
But He who marks the sparrows fall
Makes morning follow night.

He gives us courage for each need
Strength for each load we bear
He scatters all through life for us
Signs of His constant care.

He makes the rainbows shine through showers
The roses grow from rain,
He makes the winter lead to spring
And peace to follow pain.

Through all that comes His blessed Sun
Shines somewhere up above
For over all and everywhere
Is love unchanging love.

*IF I COULD ONLY WRITE A LINE*

## SOMEBODY KNOWS

Somebody knows when your heart aches
And everything seems to go wrong
Somebody knows when the shades
Need chasing away with song.

Somebody knows when you're lonely
Tired discouraged and blue
Somebody wants you to know Him
And know that he dearly loves you.

Somebody knows when you're tempted
And your mind grows dizzy and dim
Somebody cares when you're weakest
And farthest away from Him.

Somebody grieves when you're fallen
You are not lost from his sight
Somebody waits for your coming
And he'll drive the gloom from the night.

Somebody loves you when weary
Somebody loves you when strong
Always waiting to help you
He watches you one of the throng.

Needing his friendship so holy
Needing his watchcare so true
His name!  We call his name Jesus
He loves every one, he loves you.


December 20, 1940
(sent to Sister Bertha Hightower)

## SHARING

I have so many things to share
God's love, earth's beauty and the fair
And star-gemmed heavens which declare
His glory here.

I have so many things to give
The heavenly peace by which I live
And prayer's divine restorative
To bless and cheer.

I have so many things to praise
God's guidance mid life's thorny ways
His truth which lightens all my days
With luster bright.

I have so many valid signs
That God to man his ear inclines
That through the dark his mercy shines
With fadeless light.

## FRIENDSHIPS PATH

Come, let us walk down friendship's path
The way friends used to do
A winding path with daisies bright
And sparkling with the dew.

Fond memories float about the sky
Where clouds once used to be
And fairies cling to everything
Our friendship let us see.

And there we'll sing and laugh again
And cry a tear or two
We'll frick bouquets of daisies fair
I love them yet, don't you?

So smile once more and let me see
The beauty of your face
Tis' God I see in reverie
And he has loved your grace.

# CHAPTER EIGHT

# HOLIDAYS AND SEASONS

### MY NEW YEAR

I have resolved to do my best
This young New Year with all the rest
But If I will, I cannot tell
It all depends if all is well.

To boast and say this I will do
All of the days would not be true
But what I want is work and try
To overcome, not just get by.

### AT EASTER

May Jesus fold you in his arms today
And love and bless you in his richest way
On this, the day the Lord Himself has made
His light surround, his grace your soul pervade.

May he who lived and died that you might live
Move you to Him your love and life to give
This counts alone, these Paschal Joys abide
Be yours these genuine thrills of Easter tide.

Thus let me think of dear friends tried and true
So will I plead with the risen Christ for you.

*IF I COULD ONLY WRITE A LINE*

## GONE BUT NOT FORGOTTEN

While thinking of you on this Easter day
I think of those sweet songs that you used to sing
And the sweet conversation we used to have
They still live in my memory today.

Gone but not forgotten my dear
For I've thought of you often since you went away
Of how you told me you would sing in the heavenly choir some day
And those words ring in my ears today.

You were so much comfort to me my dear
While on my bed of affliction I lay
It was so sweet to know that someone thought of me
And oh, how I do miss you today.

Your presence meant so much to me
And I looked for you each day
Yes, gone but not forgotten dear
For I'm thinking of you on this Easter day.

In memory of Lucie
March 4, 1949

## THE POETRY OF MARY SOUTHERS

## DECLARATION DAY

Here's to another Declaration Day
Where many a hero is laid away
To rest until that final day
When God Himself his reward will pay.

Who fought with gun, sword, and spear
To bring a final victory near
That every man on earth should be free
And have his own liberty.

Whom God Himself did set free
When Jesus died upon the tree
To bring goodwill and peace to all mankind
That they should live in love sublime.

And someday Jesus our Captain we'll see
When his banner is unfurled
Then we'll have everlasting peace
In this sinful war torn world.

And then, only then, we shall have rest
From our labor to a just reward
And have that peace and love
Which only comes from God above.

Jesus, our Captain, who's never lost a battle
Will stand by his children today
And when this cruel life is over
He'll say, "come unto me and I will repay".

written May 24, 1944

*IF I COULD ONLY WRITE A LINE*

## ON YOUR BIRTHDAY

Beloved of my heart
Until death I shall pray
That you walk down the years
In God's gracious way.

That the lily which now
In your young heart enshrined
With the rays of his love
May forever be enshrined.

To Jesus whose beauty
Through the ages has shown
And which gleams in its whiteness
Before God's bright throne.

I give you in trust
You are young and sweet
May he keep you my darling
And guide your dear feet.

***THE POETRY OF MARY SOUTHERS***

## HAPPY BIRTHDAY

On this another birthday my dear
I've just a few words to you to say
May all the peace and happiness be yours
On this your birthday.

The Lord has been with you all the way
And has led you another mile
May he in his mercy forever keep you
As a good father does his child.

May the Lord lead and guide you
As you travel through this unfriendly world
And may you give Him the glory and thanks
And let his banner be unfurled.

written June 13, 1948

***IF I COULD ONLY WRITE A LINE***

## FATHER'S DAY

All over the world children are thinking of father
And planning gifts for Him
But I wonder how many are thinking of their heavenly father
And the gift that he gave to them that they might live.

How he gave his only son
Who was born in a manger
That by that gift all men
Should give Him their gifts in praise.

How many are giving the gift of thankfulness
For his love, guidance, and care
And through all our sorrow and trials
Our heavenly father is near.

Oh heavenly father we thank thee
Please make us humble and true to thee
And through all the pain and woes of life
May we ever be humble and thankful to thee.

For thou art the comfort of all sorrow
The giver of every good and perfect gift
Help us Oh Father to do thy will
And live in this love and bliss.

written June 18, 1944

**THE POETRY OF MARY SOUTHERS**

## ANOTHER THANKSGIVING DAY

Oh how thankful we all should be
That the Lord has spared us to see
Another glorious Thanksgiving Day
While so many others have passed away.

We should praise the Lord with all our heart
And vow to Him to never depart
For sparring us to live to see
Another glorious Thanksgiving Day

So many that have passed away
Would have loved to see this Thanksgiving Day
Then let God's spirit have its way
And praise Him for sparring us to see another Thanksgiving Day

Thank Him for shelter, for clothing and food
Thank Him for everything that is good
Thank Him for dying on the cross
So that our souls may not be lost.

written May 24, 1944

***IF I COULD ONLY WRITE A LINE***

## THANKSGIVING DAY

My grandma and ma, she said to me
These autumn leaves are sad to see
They show that winter's coming here
To lead away the weary years.

What of it, if the leaves are old
They're nice like this, all red and gold
I think the trees dress up so gay
In honor of Thanksgiving Day.

## NOTHING UNDER THE SUN

After frantic days of rushing about
In search of something new
Something modish and different
What happens to me and you?

After all this hectic effort
Trampling for blocks and blocks
We come through with the same old things
Handkerchiefs, neckties, and socks!

**THE POETRY OF MARY SOUTHERS**

## LIGHT OF THE WORLD

Over two thousand years ago today
The light first shown in this world
When Jesus Christ, our Lord, was born
Bringing light into this world on that first Christmas day.

Oh, what power there is in this light
To light the poor Pilgram's way
And if we will only follow the light
We can never loose our way.

Oh what peace and comfort there is in light
When we're on a dark and lonely road
It makes us hold our head up high
With comfort in our soul.

So let us praise and thank Him
For this Christmas day
And let His banner be unfurled
As for this wicked world of sin we pray.

That the light that shown so bright
On that beautiful Christmas day
Will shine in men's wicked souls again
For this we do pray.

written December 12, 1948

*IF I COULD ONLY WRITE A LINE*

## CHRISTMAS GREETING

When Christ down from Heaven did come to this earth
No room in the inn was there found for his birth.

So out to the stable he must go for a bed
On the hay in the manager to pillow his head.

And there mid the cattle that lay in the stall
The blessed Lord Jesus did come to us all.

Is your heart more open to the Christchild today
Is your life so full of the things for your table
That Jesus must still find a place in the stable?

Is your inn so filled up with the things of this earth
That no room is now left for His inner new birth?

Oh friend! Open thy heart. let the blessed Christ in
Allow Him to save you and free you from sin.

Let Him cast from your temple the traffic of earth
And find in your being a place for new birth.

Let him be a Christmas tree now in your heart
And never, no never, from him may you part.

## WINTER WORLD

The winter world is dressed today
In velvet robes of white
The trees encased in iciness
Whose prisons catch the light.

And flash with bits of flaming fire
Like rainbows in the sun
While every tiny twig and branch
Flaunts silver, fairy-spun.

The snow dust dances in the breeze
And drifts upon the air
Until one thinks a fairy land
Is standing jeweled there.

Oh winter has a beauty that
Is deep and wide and high
In breathless wonder man may gaze
And sense that God is nigh.

## WINTER

Glitter of frost and glamour of snow
And icicles hanging row on row
Beauty of winter that all men praise
Glory of keen and cutting days.

Winds that whistle and winds that sing
Don't be hurrying Mistress Spring
Shimmers of bare boughs under the light
Of sunshine eerie and thin and white.

Silence in forest and glen and lea
In home of beaver and hive of bee
Out an ermine robe is a robe for a string
Don't be hurrying, Mistress Spring.




It was you who set all the boundaries of the earth;
you made both summer and winter.

**Psalm 74:17**

## CHAPTER NINE

## HOPE FOR TOMORROW

### THE JOY'S OF TOMORROW

Sometimes we wonder why life's so cruel
When we have nothing but grief and sorrow
But if we'll only trust in God
It won't compare with the joys of tomorrow.

Just when we think that it all has passed
It seems that it's just begun
But if we will just trust, and be patient, and wait
Jesus will surely lead us over sin.

All through the day we shed briny tears of sorrow
And at night sorrow is so great that we can not sleep
But when we think of the mercy of God
We know, it won't compare with the joys of tomorrow.

Then we fight on through fear and trembling
Striving to keep his commandments, and do His will
For God has said, that the sorrow's of this world
Won't be compared with the joy's of tomorrow
If we will do his will.

*IF I COULD ONLY WRITE A LINE*

## WATER

Not from the rain's uncertain pool
Do cattle quench their thirst
For beasts must have a second drought
Where they have found their first.

And so the herdsmen seek a spring
In some green tranquil vale
Knowing though summer suns beat hot
Its water cannot fail.

Oh soul of man with all thy thirst
If thou would drink thy fill
Thou too can find a living stream.
That gushes from a hill.

So leave earth's brief and shallow pools
That vanish or grow stale
And seek the one Eternal Spring
Whose waters never fail.

If thine enemy be hungry, give him bread to eat;
and if he be **thirsty**, give him water to drink:

**Proverbs 25:21**

## *THE POETRY OF MARY SOUTHERS*

## SOMEDAY WE'LL UNDERSTAND

Let's walk together hand in hand
As we travel through this barren land
And when we reach the portal ff the promised land
Then we all shall understand.

Sometimes the way is so dark and dreary
And our trials are so hard to bear
But if we'll just hold fast to Jesus hand
Someday we'll understand.

For Jesus knows all about us
And He sees all things and understands
And when we get home to Jesus
He'll make it plain and then we'll understand.

Trials may come on every hand
And why we cannot understand
But our dsear Savior will see us through
And he'll help us to understand.

written July 18, 1944

## THERE IS A HOME

Upon the hill there is a home
Where weary travelers cease to roam.
Which God Himself has prepared
That His inheritance with Him may share.

Which has suffered pain and sorrow too
Whose journey was trials and burdens through
But alas, the journey was complete
Upon the hill of Jerusalem's Street.

And someday we too will meet our journeys end
And will meet again our dear friends
With them to be forever and to part no more
Upon that Hill inside Heavens door.

God help us each day to prepare
To reach that home that's over there
For those who've been washed in the blood of the lamb
That we may be with Thee at God's right hand.

For he said that He was going to prepare
A mansion for his children over there
That where He is that we might be
And have life all through eternity.

## WHEN WILL I KNOW

I do not know, nor can I tell
When the face of Christ I shall see
But I am sure and I know so well
One of these days I am going home.

When will I see and how can I tell
What mine eyes some day shall see
But I am sure, Oh I know quite well
To live with Jesus how happy I will be.

When will I know, how can I tell
When he calls me to my home above
Redeemed through his atoning blood
I am sheltered in my Savior's love.

"It is well, yes, with my soul, I know"
And the gates stand ajar for me
To give an entrance to that city fair
Where loved ones are waiting for me there.

*IF I COULD ONLY WRITE A LINE*

## STRENGTH TO BEAR

As we struggle along life's lonely way
Burdened down with sorrow and care
When we feel that we can no farther go
Then Jesus gives us strength to bear.

When our way is dark and dreary
And it seems that nobody seems to care
Then with tear blinded eyes, yes we pray to God.
For just a little more strength to bear.

Oh I'm so glad that there is one
That will give us strength to bear
For Jesus has promised not to leave us alone
But all of our burdens to share.

Sometimes we wonder why life's so cruel
And our cross seems so heavy to bear
But Jesus told us to pick up our cross
And he'd give us strength to bear.

And when we think of the sunshine just ahead
In that land so bright and fair
It gives us strength to bear life's toils
And someday his glory we'll share.


written  November 14, 1948

## THE POETRY OF MARY SOUTHERS

## CHEER UP

Cheer up, my friend, don't be blue
Your heavenly father cares for you
And when you feel sad and feel blue
Just remember that your dear Savior was sad too.

When we are burdened down with pain
Just remember our Savior went through the same
But let us cheer up in Jesus name.

There is not a pain that he don't understand
For he bore the same in his fist and hands
His body was in pain from head to foot
So let's cheer up, don't worry but look.

We may have sorrow that is true
But our dear Savior had sorrow too
When he prayed in the Garden he was sorrowful unto death
But he suffered until his work was through.

And when his burden was so heavy, he looked up you see
And said father, "if it is thy will let this cup pass from me.
Not my will but Thine be done
For it was for this cause into this world I came"

So let it be sorrow or it may be pain
Help us Dear Lord to bear in Jesus name
So let's cheer up and forever pray
That as he did, we too, will overcome some day.

written Oct. 22, 1944, 3:00 a.m.

*IF I COULD ONLY WRITE A LINE*

## WELL DONE

In this blessed pilgrim journey
We may often meet with pain
But the hand of Jesus holds us
Through the sunshine and the rain.

When the day is filled with trials
Jesus fills the night with song
And he holds our hand the tightest
When the battle rages strong.

He has led me o'er the mountains
When the way seemed blocked and barred
He has brought me through the desert
When the way was dry and hard.

I can trust Him for the future
Though the way be rough and wild
He has promised grace sufficient
To his weary helpless child.

When the winter wind is blowing
And the frost is on my head
I shall reach my hand to Jesus
With no lurking sense of dread.

With my life's work all completed
Though no earthly gain I've won,
It will be enough to pay me
Just to hear Him say, "Well done".

### *THE POETRY OF MARY SOUTHERS*

## HAPPY AT LAST

We are oftentimes burdened with sorrow
And our cross seems too heavy to bear
But if we hold the hand of Jesus
He has promised our burdens to share.

Though our lives be sometimes dreary
Trouble may be on every hand
But if we serve and trust the master
He will give us grace to stand.

Great trials and tribulations
May be all along the way
But by the grace of Jesus
We will be free some day.

Our hearts are sometimes burdened
And our eyes shed briny tears,
But when we go on to Jesus
He drives away our doubts and fears.

He has promised to bear our burdens
If we do his will and keep his command
He has promised never to leave us
But see us to the promised land.

So, let us fight on like brave soldiers
Till the strife of life has past
Then we'll be free from our burdens
And we will be with Jesus at last.

Then we will be happy in his presence
All burdens and sorrows past
When we shall be in God's kingdom
Then we shall be free, and happy at last.

*Mary Southers first poem*

*IF I COULD ONLY WRITE A LINE*

**THE POETRY OF MARY SOUTHERS**

# BOOK II
# IF I COULD ONLY WRITE A LINE

*The Religious and Inspirational
Poetry Of Mary Southers*

*Selected & Edited by
Charles C. Hagan, Jr.*

*IF I COULD ONLY WRITE A LINE*

# CONTENTS
# BOOK II

Chapter Ten
**PRAISE, ADORATION & WORSHIP**   119
    Elevation, The Savior Is Born, A Lesson, His Choice, White Rose, At Lent, Christ's Birthday, With Him Eternally, The Sun, Moon & The Stars, The Martyr, Mary's Flower, With Thee Above, We Thank Our Dear Father, In A Little Town, Called Bethlehem, The Holy Family, Dear Mother of Jesus, Upon The Hill of Calvary, Dear Mother of Jesus, Nazareth Workshop, This Is My Body, The Shepherds Adore The Infant Savior, The Good Old Fashioned Way, The Angelus, He Was Led To Calvary, Upon The Hill of Calvary, The Trees Birds & The Air, The Trees, Corpus Christi, God The Supreme Being, For Me He Came, The Best Things Come In Threes

Chapter Eleven
**PRAYERS**   143
    The Hay, Lord We Thank Thee, Dear Lord I Cannot Make My Way, Oh God Help Me, Battlefield Prayer For Peace, God We Thank Thee, Prayer, Faith, In Everything Give Thanks, Oh Lord I'm So Thankful, Dear Lord I Thank You, Lord We're So Thankful That We Have You, God Pity Us Afraid, Oh I'm So Thankful

Chapter Twelve
**FRIENDSHIP**   157
    Love Thy Neighbor, As I Sit Alone, To A Faraway Love, You, To A Friend, To Light My Way, Sentiments of Home, Sweetheart Of Jesus, Oh Love That Will Not Let Thee Go

Chapter Thirteen
**INSPIRATIONAL**   163
    More Time, Bonds, Consistency, Just Wait On The Lord, Live For Something, Lonely Star, My Best-Second Prize, The Smiling Fool, Through The Window, Practical, He Suffered That We Might Live, Evening Thought, Will He Have Time For You, Let's Go Forward, My Guardian Angel, The Power Of God, Has The Light Grown Dim, Just Jesus And Me, Promises Of Our Lord, Peter's Bark, Valley of Humiliation, Cheer Up, When Will I Know

*THE POETRY OF MARY SOUTHERS*

Chapter Fourteen
**MOTHER, FATHER, & CHILDREN** 183
    Thankful for Mother, The Arms of Mother Earth, Father's Pride,
    Little Brother, Mother of Jesus, Lean Upon My Arms Mother,
    In Memory-She Served The Lord In Word & Deed, Mother,
    Dearest Mother, Mother's Day,, Dear Mother, Bless Thou Me Oh Mother


## OTHER UNPUBLISHED POEMS BY MARY SOUTHERS

Special Attention, My Nuptial Day, The Hidden Garden, Take In The Slacks, Scissors, To Christ Our Lord, Meeting, With Mary Magdelene, The Image of Death, Our Lady of The Way, The Poor Box, The God That Rules, Christ, Crucified, A Young Mother, A Prayer For Dad, Baby Mine, Departed Joy, The Lost Sheep, To The Faithful Departed, Upon Your Heart, Valentine of Violets, In Memory of Rev. J.M. Williams, Jesus Is There, God Our King, The Lord Bless Thee, Mother of Sorrow, As I Look Back Over The Hill, My Mother, Breakfast At Grandpa's, Old Fashioned Mother, Mother of Jesus, School Day Memories, Fault Finders, Gone But Not Forgotten, Windows of the Soul, Chatter Box, Lullaby Lady, No More Until Morning, The Annunciation, Light of The World, There Is A Home, The Babe of Bethlehem, Mother of Mine, Christmas Greeting, Thus Saith The Lord, Youth, He's Not Here, Little Flower, Mother of Jesus, To Light My Way, Real Friendship, Weeping

*IF I COULD ONLY WRITE A LINE*

# CHAPTER TEN

# PRAISE, ADORATION, & WORSHIP

### ELEVATION

God lifts the sun
Aloft for us to see
And chaliced ocean
Holds with potent hand.

But greater still
Allows himself to be
In Cup and Host
Upheld as men demand.

### THE SAVIOR IS BORN

God rest you merry gentlemen
Let nothing you dismay
For Jesus Christ our Savior
Was born upon this day.

To save us all from Satan's power
When we were gone astray
Oh tidings of comfort and joy
For Jesus Christ our Savior was born on Christmas day.

## A LESSON

As deep mid dreary wooded hills
A brooklet formed by hidden rills
Reflects the sunshine of the sky
That steals through withered leaves on high.

So let each gloomy day of strife
That passes in this vale of life
Reflect the joys that are above
The sunshine of eternal love.

## HIS CHOICE

One flower likes the dew
And will drink it up
That taste of heaven through
Its open cup.

A flower that will close
Loses of the dew
And that is why God chose
One of the two.

## WHITE ROSE

A saw a white rose
Born this morn
My fingers were its stem
Christ lips by mine
Spoke words of life
And silent wheat obeyed.

And I am sure his mother smiled
To see her son repose
A white rose on white linen
as once at Bethlehem.

I saw a white rose
Born this morn
My fingers were its stem.


## AT LENT

How speedy were the months that passed
With all their sorrow, joy, and pain
And now for forty days we fast
Until Our Lord shall come again.

How small a sacrifice, tis true
To honor him who fasted first
How little is this thing we do
To him, who dying said, "I thirst".

*IF I COULD ONLY WRITE A LINE*

## CHRIST'S BIRTHDAY

Oh what love that God had for us
When he gave his only begotten son
To be born for us in such a lowly way
For the last and fallen one.

Then suffered and died
Upon the cross
And paid the debt
So that we may not be lost.

What a glorious morn it was to the world
When in the manger he did lay
When Mary had wrapped him in swaddling cloth
And laid him in the bed of hay.

He so willingly left his home on high
To be born in a manger then afterward die
Then Christmas was in heaven o're the return of God's son
Who suffered such a death on the cross
But the victory he won.

He brought peace to the world
And good will to all mankind
And with him came our Christmas day
That we should all remember well
That it is Jesus' birthday.

Then how sacred it should be kept
With joy and mirth and love
For bringing to us this Christmas day.
From heaven up above.

## WITH HIM ETERNALLY

Joseph our certain hope of life
Glory of earth and heaven
Thou pillar of the world to thee
Be praise eternal given.

There as salvation's minister
The mighty maker chose
As foster father of the world
As Mary's spotless spouse.

With joy thou sawest him new born
Of whom the prophets sang
Him in a manger did adore
For whom creation sprang.

The Lord of Lords and King of King
Ruler of sky and sea
Whom heaven and earth and hell obey
Was subject unto thee.

Blessed Trinity vouchsafe to us
Through Joseph's merits high
To mount the heavenly seats and reign
With him eternally.

*IF I COULD ONLY WRITE A LINE*

## THE SUN, MOON AND THE STARS

The sun moon and the star's
What a wonderful part they did play
When the word of the prophet was fulfilled
That a savior would be born to save the world
While the world lay quiet and still.

The moon lit the way of the shepherd's
While they were watching over the sheep
The star led them to the manger
Where the darling Christ child did sleep.

The sun with all of its splendor
Glittered all over the world so bright that day
Telling all the world what a blessing had come
When Christ our Lord was born that first Christmas day.

The sun moon and stars rejoiced that day
And the angels sang all over the world
And when the shepherds saw the star they too began to sing
Glory to the newborn King.

The sun moon and stars did rejoice
The oxen worshipped him too with the wise men
And with one accord they all did sing
Glory in the highest to the newborn King.

Even the oxen's joined with that glorious song
With the angels the shepherd and wise men
With their voices blending in with one accord
Peace on earth good will toward men!

## THE MARTYR

As Adam walked in paradise
He found a little violet
All crushed and broken by a foot
But still not withered yet.

"Poor little thing, who walked on thee
Whose foot hath on thee trod?"
But the flower happily cried
"The foot was that of God".

## MARY'S FLOWER

The manger was a flower pot
In which the infant Jesus grew
And Mary's sweet forget-me-not
Looked up into her eyes of blue.

The flower flourished and in time
His father took with him a sigh
And put him on the cross to climb
That he could be with him on high.

*IF I COULD ONLY WRITE A LINE*

## WITH THEE ABOVE

While with ceaseless course the sun
Hastens through the former year
Many souls their races have run
Nevermore to meet us here.

Fixed in our eternal state
They have done with all below
We little longer wait
But how little, none can know

As the winged arrow flies
Speedily the mark to find
As the lighting from the skies
Darts and leaves no trace behind.

Swiftly thus our fleeting days
Bear us down life's rapid stream
Upward Lord our spirits rise
All below is but a dream.

Thanks for mercies past received
Pardon of our sins renew
Teach us henceforth how to live
With eternity in view.

Bless thy word to young and old
Fill us with out Savior's love
And when life's short tale is told
May we dwell with thee above.

### *THE POETRY OF MARY SOUTHERS*

## WE THANK OUR DEAR FATHER ABOVE

H e was born in a manger among the beast
That our trembling souls he might release
From the pit of hell to which they were doomed
But still when he came there was no room.

He so willingly left his home on high
To be born in a manger then to die
That by his death that we might live
And then be with him on high.

There was joy in heaven
O're the return of God's son
Who suffered such a death on the cross
But the victory he won.

Merry Christmas and a Happy New Year
God bless you and pray for me.


To Mr and Mrs Venela Wilson
from Mrs Mary Southers.

*IF I COULD ONLY WRITE A LINE*

## IN A LITTLE TOWN CALLED BETHLEHEM

In a little town called Bethlehem
Many many years ago
There was a little baby born
To be the Savior of men.

He was despised and hated by the world
But he loved them just the same
And he died a horrible death on the tree
That they might be saved by his name.

Though shamefully treated here on earth by men
He knew that his work on earth was through
And he said, "Father forgive them
For they know not what they do".

Even while dying on the cross
The thief repented and said
"Lord when thou comest into thy kingdom
Please remember me".

And Jesus heard his pitiful cry
And through his suffering, he said
"I say unto you that this day
Thou shall be with me in paradise".

written Dec. 15, 1947 @ 3:00 a.m.

***THE POETRY OF MARY SOUTHERS***

## THE HOLY FAMILY

Glad in the folk it cheriseth
That august home of Nazareth
Where first the holy church unfurled
Her banners o're the expectant world.

The sun that greets the peaceful earth
With golden light at each day's birth
Hath seen since first his course he trod
No happier home than this of God.

Here gather oft with guardian eye
God's messengers from courts on high
They love to hoover around the place
The sanctuary of good and grace.

Ah with what reverent careful skill
Works Christ his foster father's will
And with what joy in heart and eyes
The maid her mother love supplies.

Partner in love in care allied
Stands Joseph by his spouse's side
Grace from the fount of good imparts
A thousand bonds to link their hearts.

So love the twain in bond complete
And both their loves in Jesus meet
And to them both doth he afford
Of mutual love the fair reward.

Oh that like love of equal might
Would us in one for age unite
And bringing household peace o'ercome
Life woes in every earthly home.

***IF I COULD ONLY WRITE A LINE***

## DEAR MOTHER OF JESUS

Dear mother of Jesus how I do adore you
For your darling son that was brought in this world
As a ransom for this wicked world
Who's soul's was lost, that brought us back to God.

We thank God that he found favor in thee
That you should be the mother of his son
That through you, he should come into this world
That God's will would be done.

Oh mother of Jesus how we do love thee
The greatest mother in all the world
May we forever be humble and thankful to God
And let his banner be unfurled.

Oh mother of Jesus what pain you must have borne
To see your son treated so
But through God's divine love
That you are happy now forever more.

written February 13, 1946

*THE POETRY OF MARY SOUTHERS*

## NAZARETH WORKSHOP

Oh Joseph humble carpenter
Your shop held priceless treasures
Just bits of wood tis true but they
Were blest beyond all measure.

For these same bits were touched by hands
That hold life and eternity
The precious hands of Jesus for
He helped you labor, didn't he?

## THIS IS MY BODY

This is my body
Oh sacrifice,
Oh crimson flood
Eyes has not seen nor ear has heard
The glory which came
At your solemn word.

My school boy lad
With the sun kissed hair
What powers you have
How can I dare
To ask your prayers
For me to him, I seek the new Jerusalem.

*IF I COULD ONLY WRITE A LINE*

## THE SHEPHERDS ADORE THE INFANT SAVIOR

Come we shepherds whose blessed sight
Hath met loves moon in nature's might
Come lift we up our loftier song
And wake the Son that lies to long.

We saw Thee in Thy balmy nest
Young dawn of our eternal day
We saw thine eyes break from their east
And chase the trembling shades away.

We saw Thee and we blessed the sight
We saw thee by thine own sweet sight.

Welcome all wonders in one sight
Eternity shut in a span
Summers in winter, day in might
Heaven in earth and God in man.

Great little one whose all-embracing birth
Lifts earth to heaven, stoops heaven to earth
To thee meek majesty soft shing
Of simple graces and sweet loves.

Each of us his lamb will bring
Each his pair of silver doves
Till burned at last in fire of Thy fair eyes
Ourselves become our own best sacrifice.

## THE ANGELUS

In a valley fair, a lovely scene
    Aglow with setting sun
The west alive with golden light
    Proclaims the day is done.

A silver ribbon winds among
    Rich fields of emerald green
The earth takes on the eerie hue
    Of sunset's golden sheen.

Then from a slender silent spire
    That upward points to sky
Ring out sweet chimes, a mellow call
    To turn our thoughts on high.

And in each hamlet, burg, and town
    We see devout souls pause
With humbled head and tranquil men
    United in one cause.

To hail the queen of heaven and earth
    The mother of our soul
And thank the Lord of heaven her son
    For giving us a goal!

*IF I COULD ONLY WRITE A LINE*

## HE WAS LED TO CALVARY

On that dark and lonely night
The lamb of God was led
And on that rough and rugged cross
His precious blood was shed.

Left all alone he faced that cruel mob
That had condemned him to die
He went to the cross with out a word
To die for you and I.

It was such love that he had for us
That he bore such pain and shame
He was led to Calvary for our redemption
The we might live through his holy name.

We thank you heavenly father for your dear Son
That was led with shame to Calvary
To die such a horrible death on the cross
For such a sinner as I that was lost.

Who on the third day did arise
The savior with victory
With the keys of death hell and the grave
That will set all men free.

And he said, "come unto me
All ye that are burdened and I will give you rest
Take up your cross and follow me"
Along the road too Calvary.

Dear God please help us to be true too you
For the pain and suffering that you went through
When you hung up on the cross and died
And for our sins was crucified.

## UPON THE HILL OF CALVARY

When I think about the hill of Calvary
Oh what memories I do see
How my blessed savior bled and died
For such a wretched sinner as you and me.

When I think of the shame that he bore
When he hung between the murderer and the thief
On the hill of Calvary upon the tree
Suffering bleeding and dying for sinners like you and me.

Sometimes I tremble when I think
Of what he went through for you and me
But I rejoice to know that he loves me
When I think of the hill of Calvary.

When I feel lonely and forsaken
Somehow my burdens seem lighter
When I think of the hill of Calvary
Where Jesus died for me.

written 5:00 a.m. Feb. 18, 1946

And when they were come to the place, which is called **Calvary**
there they crucified him, and the malefactors,
one on the right hand, and the other on the left.

**Luke 23:33**

*IF I COULD ONLY WRITE A LINE*

## THE TREES, THE BIRDS AND THE AIR

Oh what emblem that we can see in trees
As we think of Calvary
For it was there that Jesus bed and died
When he hung upon the tree.

He gave his life upon the tree
That we poor sinners might live
Then let us glory in the cross
And look to him and live.

Even the little birds find glory in the trees
For it is there that they find their home
And with their songs give thanks to GOD
For shelter in the trees.

And when the balmy air does blow
Among the fluttering leaves
What a blessing it is that we can share
The glory in the tree's the birds and the air.

written June 30th 1946 3:15 a.m.

### ***THE POETRY OF MARY SOUTHERS***

## TREES

Oh what beauty there is in trees
That God himself has created with his own hand
And afterwards he gave his only begotten son
To be hung upon a tree, for the redemption of man.

Whenever we look at a tree we should always see
The suffering and agony that he went through for you and me
When he left his home on high with such love
To die upon Calvary's hill upon the tree.

Dear Lord we thank thee for the tree
That with thine own hand thou planted for me
That your dear son gave his life as a sacrifice
That we poor sinners might be free.

Take my life dear Lord and let it be
Consecrated forever unto thee
May we live so that we can tell others of your love
That you gave to the world when you died upon the tree.

written February 15, 1948

## CORPUS CHRISTI

As pure and still as star bright foam
Upon some dim and silent sea
White lilies deck God's earthly home
Where now his children bend the knee.

O Lord reveal thy hidden face
My JESUS may this hour of grace
Be love's eternity to me.

And on this high and holy feast
I see the bread of angels shine
What joy to kneel before his priest
To feel and know all heaven is mine.

O Lord reveal thy hidden face
My Jesus in this hour of grace
My life is linked with life divine.

Yes thou art mine —no angel choir
Receives a gift so great and free
My being thrills with sacred fire
United Oh my Lord to thee.

Now Lord thy hast revealed thy face
My Jesus in this hour of grace
When love gives love himself to me

## THE POETRY OF MARY SOUTHERS

## GOD THE SUPREME BEING

God, the supreme being made the world and all there is
He made man after his own likeness and image
Regardless to race or color we're all his children
We are all human beings.

If men would only see each other as human beings
And not as just another man
Then there would be real brother hood in the world
For we are all human beings.

Jesus' last commandment that he gave to his disciples
Was to love one another as I have loved you
So if we will only see each other as human beings
Then real peace and love will be among men.

We should love and feel each other's care
Regardless to rich or poor
For Jesus died for the whole round world
What man could have done more?

He, the supreme being, laid down his life
That we human beings might live
And if we as his followers would only be true
Then heaven would be on earth with hearts pure and clean
For God's the father of all human beings.

We should not look at each other as those wicked men did Jesus
Just as a man, and said, "Away with him,
We'll not have him rule over us
For they could not see beyond the man
And see the Supreme being, their Lord and Savior.

written December 1945

*IF I COULD ONLY WRITE A LINE*

## FOR ME HE CAME

For me He left his home on high
For me to earth He came to die
For me He in a manger lay
For me to Egypt fled away.

For me He dwelt with fishermen
For one He dwelt in cave and glen
For me abuse He meekly bore
For me a crown of thrns He wore.

For me He braved Gethsemane
For me He hung upon a tree
For me His final feast was made
For me by Judas was betrayed.

For me by Peter was denied
For me by Pilate crucified
For me His precious blood was shed
For me He slept among the dead.

For me He rose with might at last
For me above the skies He passed
For me He came at God's command
For me He sits at His right hand.

**THE POETRY OF MARY SOUTHERS**

## THE BEST THING'S COME IN THREES

The best things that the world has ever received
When God himself created the world
In the trinity there was the three, I am told
God the Father, Son, and the Holy Ghost, the three.

When the Christ child was born that first Christmas day
In the stable the manger in such a lowly way
In his tiny little face you could see
God the Father, the Son, the Holy Ghost, the three.

Although a little babe his face did shine
And the suffering that he had to go through had not come
He bore the image of his heavenly father divine
And they knew that he was God's son.

And when that cruel day did come
And the victory he had won on the cross
Then the best gift that was ever given to the world
Was God the Father, Son and the Holy Ghost.

There's nothing that can be done without the three
For they go together you see
Oh how rich we are to be heir's to the throne
God the Father, the Son, and the Holy Ghost.

## IF I COULD ONLY WRITE A LINE

*THE POETRY OF MARY SOUTHERS*

# CHAPTER ELEVEN

# PRAYERS

### THE HAY

The hay in the manger cradled them
Mary and Jesus in Bethlehem.

Cradled them closely mother and child
Born of the spirit undefiled.

Cradled them sweetly one with the other
Jesus the child, Mary the mother.

Lord may I be humbly the hay
Cradling the child and mother today?

***IF I COULD ONLY WRITE A LINE***

## LORD WE THANK THEE

Dear Lord we thank thee for such love
That was wrapped up in flesh and sent from above
That we poor mortals might be free
To give humble and sincere thnks to thee.

We thank thee for the love that you gave
When you hung upon the cross so gallant and brave
That every creature might be free
To give thee glory and thanks to thee.

Oh God help us to keep our eyes on thee
The only hope of victory
That by the power all men may see
That with thee all things can be.

We thank thee for shelter, clothes and food
We thank thee for everything that's good
But above all dear God we thank thee most
For your darling son who died for us on the cross.

## THE POETRY OF MARY SOUTHERS

## DEAR LORD, I CANNOT MAKE MY WAY

Oh Lord, please help me I pray
To look to you from day to day
For there are so many changes in this world today
That I cannot make my way.

Dear Jesus, please help me to look to thee
The only one that can show me the way
For without you, dear Lord, I will fail
Alone I cannot make my way.

Though pain and sorrow fill my soul
To you I will always pray
For thou knowest all things, dear Lord
And thou alone can make my way.

Oh help me dear Lord to lean on thee
Who has planned my way for me
For if I tried Dear Lord, I never could
Make my way without thee.

written Sept. 19, 1945

## OH GOD HELP ME

Oh lord a lost sinner that I am
Please help me to understand
How that you died for me on the cross
That my soul may not be lost.

Oh Jesus please open my eyes and let me see
The horrible death you paid for me
That by your death I might live
And have life more abundantly.

Oh lord please help me, I pray
Please take my trembling hand
And give me grace to trust thee
Oh dear God have mercy on me
And help me before its too late to understand.

Don't turn him away today I pray
For he is the way, the truth, and the light
For he said hear my voice today, harden not your heart
For tomorrow may be too late, ye may die

What profit a man to gain the whole world
And then lose his own soul
When a man loses his soul, he has lost all
Why not take Jesus and live?  God help me!

***THE POETRY OF MARY SOUTHERS***

## BATTLEFIELD PRAYER FOR PEACE

Let us in peace O master walk with thee
While foes of thine we fight on battlefield
Thy beacon light do thou let shine that we
In darkness may not unto Satan yield.

And this our battle cry always shall be
To none but thee oh master let us yield
We have no fear oh master when with thee
Arraigned on cruel grim dark battlefield.

Then lead us on as only one in thee
And peace divine shall reign on battlefield
And thus to thee our prayer shall always be
From foes of Thine do thou oh master yield.

The LORD shall fight for you,
and ye shall hold your **peace**.

**Exodus 14:14**

*IF I COULD ONLY WRITE A LINE*

## GOD WE THANK THEE

Great God we thank thee for this home
This bounteous birth land of the free
Where strangers from afar may come
And breathe the air of liberty.

Long may her flowers untrammeled spring
Her harvests wave, her cities rise
And yet till time shall fold her wing
Remain earth's loveliest paradise.

Yea heaven is the prize
My soul shall strive to gain
One glimpse of paradise
Repairs a life of pain.

Yes heaven is the prize
Death opens wide the door
And then the spirit flies
To God for evermore.

## PRAYER

If you think in me Jesus
My thoughts will be clear as dew
If you speak out of me Jesus
My words will be kind and true.

If you work in me, Oh Jesus
My deeds will be doubly blest
Sanctified be all my labor
Hallowed ever be my rest.

Till then Jesus, all my being
All I think and say and do
Until my whole life shall mirror
The great loving heart of you.


## FAITH

He will not leave me here to die
Forsaken and alone
Who never yet has passed me by
Just like the rose, unblown.

He will not leave me face to face
With death's relentless foe
Who gave the roses Mary's grace
Because he loved her so.

He will not leave me to my fate
Whatever it may be
Who can the rose make flower late
More beautiful to see.

*IF I COULD ONLY WRITE A LINE*

## IN EVERYTHING GIVE THANKS

In everything give thanks!

When bread in fullness is thy daily store
When near thy dwelling comes no plague nor blight
When boding ills forecast no coming night
When to thy riches each day addeth more.

Say not, "My hand hath gotten me this wealth"
Remember who it is that gives thee power
The cunning hand and brain,
The glow of health.

Receive thou humbly as God's free-will dower
To boasting give no place
Thine own is all of grace
In everything give thanks.

In everything give thanks
When fail the flocks and heards and fields are bare
When lips need press the bitter cup of pain
When each days close marks loss where once was gain.

Oh troubled soul, remember in thy care
The Master took the symbols of his death
With thanks he broke the bread
And poured the wine

Scourged Paul and Silas praised with every breath
Habakkuk's field more barren than thine
Despair not, trust and pray
Commit to God thy way
In everything give thanks.

*THE POETRY OF MARY SOUTHERS*

## OH LORD I'M SO THANKFUL

Dear Lord I am so thankful for mother
And I am also thankful for her love
For your love and care dear Lord and mother
Are the best friends I ever had.

I'm so thankful for such a mother
Who taught me about Jesus and his love
And taught me to pray and seek Jesus
That I might live with him in heaven above.

I thank you for life dear Father
And for health that I may earn my daily bread
And for the home that you prepared for me in glory
On the cross when your precious blood was shed.

May I forever walk in your footsteps
Please touch me the way of the cross
Help me to live so that I can tell others
How that you died that we might not be lost.

written October 2nd, 1947

*IF I COULD ONLY WRITE A LINE*

## DEAR LORD, I THANK YOU

I have no mansion, I have no wealth
But I thank you dear Lord for health
I have no diamonds to wear on my hand
I have no cars, I have no land
Expensive clothes I have none
No wondrous deeds have I ever done.

But I thank you for dying on the cross
For suffering so that I may not be lost
I thank you for this immeasurable love
I thank you for all dear Lord above.

I thank you for the birds, the trees
For beautiful lakes and cooling breeze
For the grass, the flowers, the moon, the sun
For restful evening when day's work is done.

For letting me take you to my unworthy heart
Stay with me dear Lord, please never depart.
I know my worldly possessions are few
But for all your blessings, dear Lord, I thank you.

## THE POETRY OF MARY SOUTHERS

## LORD WE'RE SO THANFUL THAT WE HAVE YOU

In this world there is nothing certain today
And at times we just don't know what to do
But deep down in our hearts we are so thankful
Dear Lord that we still have you.


We may be denied of this world's goods
We may be buffed about and scored too
But you said dear Lord that all power's in your hands
And we're so thankful that we still have you.

For you said that you'd take care of those that trust you
Although sometimes we get weak and weary too
But somehow you always see us through dear Lord
And we're so glad dear Lord that we still have you.

Dear Lord please make us thankful
And help us to serve you true
For though we may lose all we have in this world
Dear Lord we're so thankful that we still have you.


written Nov. 18th, 1948

*IF I COULD ONLY WRITE A LINE*

## GOD PITY US AFRAID

There is no health in stars
There is no healing in all the winds of night
No answer to the lifted hands
Appealing refuge from fright.

Detached brutality of power
Goes grinding the unresisting bone
Pressing the impotent grape of flesh
Nor minding what wine drops down alone.

God you must hear us now
You must awaken
There is no God but you
Now that the great wheel turn
Our faith is shaken, in what our flesh held true.

Not Isis, nor Moloch, or Nile
Nor the sun can save us
From horrow we have made
We have lost the sign, forgotten
The word you gave us
God pity us afraid.

**THE POETRY OF MARY SOUTHERS**

## OH, I'M SO THANKFUL

Oh I'm so thankful that Jesus sees and knows
All that befalls us along life's dreary way
And if we'll just have patience and wait on God
He'll brighten the way someday.

When it seems that the way is hedged up on every side
That we don't know which way to turn
Oh Lord I'm so thankful to thee
For you told us to take up thy yoe and learn.

Old Satn fights so hard sometimes
That it seems I can hardly stand
But when I think of how thathe fought Jesus our Savior
Oh I'm so thankful I'm holding to his mighty hand.

No matter how hard Satan fights us
Jesus is always standing by to see
Then someday he'll give us the victory, if we only wait
Then down in our hearts we can say
Oh Lord I'm so thankful to thee.

Dear Lord help us to look past Satan
And see you standing by
Ready and able to fight our battles
Then let us say, Oh Lord, I'm so thankful to thee
Nothing else matters now.

finished August 28th, 1949

*IF I COULD ONLY WRITE A LINE*

## CHAPTER TWELVE

## FRIENDSHIP

### LOVE THY NEIGHBOR

"Love thy neighbor"
If men would listen dear God
Their blood would not be crimsoning the sod.

If the world, dear God,
Would obey your command
There'd be peace and happiness in every land.

"Love thy neighbor"!!
Men turn a deafened ear
Your second greatest commandment they will not hear.

Love thy neighbor! Dear God
You plead near and far, men laugh in your face
And march to hell called "War"!

*IF I COULD ONLY WRITE A LINE*

## AS I SIT ALONE

As I sit alone dear Lord I think of thee
How lonely you were when your friends left thee
To bear the heavy load all alone
But thou did win the victory.

Through all your sorrow and loneliness
You toiled on unto the bitter end
Although they left you did not leave them
And at last you saved them in the end.

Help me dear lord regardless how dark it may seem to me
To look to thee for comfort and help I plead
For I know that all my help comes from thee
For you promised never to leave me.

I know dear master that you're the only friend I have
And with you nothing seems to be so bad
For I know that I'll serve and trust thee
That someday my heart will be made glad.

written Jan 9, 1949

### THE POETRY OF MARY SOUTHERS

## TO A FARAWAY LOVE

Home is where the heart is
Someone said long ago
How true this is I had not thought
before-but now I know.

Though you wonder far away
Wherever you may be
Since all my heart goes there with you
That place is home to me.

## YOU

Somewhere in the divine plan
The Master has chiseled with care
A stately niche
With peculiar curves and arch
Which no one can fill but you.

Sometime in this wonderful scheme
The Master will await an artist rare
To grace the niche
Who will play this role with ease.

God grant it will be someone I know-you.

*IF I COULD ONLY WRITE A LINE*

## TO A FRIEND

You whose heart throbs to a heart divine
Oh come, come teach this heart of mine
To thrill to tempo true and sweet
That marks divinity's our beat.

To rest my head upon Christ's breast
Beloved by the love's heart at rest
You whose heart throbs to a heart divine
So teach this yearning heart of mine.

## TO LIGHT MY WAY

There was a light of heaven in her smile
A radiance fling to her from some sweet isle
Of rest to light the long last weary mile.

"I have outlived my usefulness, you know"
She whispered, "And am very glad to go"
I never knew a smile to touch me so.

Old people should not ever think that they
Have passed their usefulness a single day
While they can smile at one in such a way.

A smile that proves a brave unselfish heart
A smile that can pure faith in life impart
Tells more than our letters and our art.

I think that smile will always with us stay
Will light my heart until my dying day.

*THE POETRY OF MARY SOUTHERS*

## SENTIMENTS OF HOME

To be a great success
Man must impart
The best of all he owns
To just one art.

Great men may learn about
Science and law
Who wear an outer badge
With loud applause.

Some men make humble home
Successful art
And wear a badge of love
Upon their heart.


## SWEETHEART OF JESUS

I was a lost soul in a world full of pain
I stumbled and stumbled and stumbled again
Bt then my eyes opened to a beckoning light
I know it will guide me through a long happy life.

Sweetheart of Jesus with a love so true
Sweetheart of Jesus how I adore you
My savior from heaven God sent you one day
To die for us sinners and to **take sin away.**

Oh help me to carry my share of the cross
So the life I am living won't add up for loss.
I need you my Jesus each step of the way
To guide me to heaven on that great judgment day.

*IF I COULD ONLY WRITE A LINE*

## LOVE THAT WILL NOT LET THEE GO

Oh love that will not let thee go
Help us this day to sing
The song that the angels sang
Hosanna, to the newborn King.

He who left his home on high
To lay in the manger of hay
And when the shepherds saw the star
And they came to worship him that day.

Oh love that will not let thee go
Dear God please help us to be true to you
For the pain and suffering that you went through
When you hung upon the cross and died
And for our sins was crucified.

## CHAPTER THIRTEEN

## /INSPIRATION

### MORE TIME

I don't have to hurry like the atheist
For I have more time than he
He just has till the day he dies
But I have eternity.


### BONDS

Of hewn rock, tall and grand
I saw a Cathedral stand
In classic beauty
Against the wear of time.

Throughout the years it stands
Each part a rock
Without beauty without meaning
The whole a house of God.

I pray that through the years
The bonds between us holds unbroken
Steadfast like the mortar that unites the rock
And endures imaging in that old old church.

## CONSISTENCY

Unto thy best be true
And let each noble thought
In action show its perfect counterpart.

God judges the intentions true
For God alone
Can read the human heart.

Unto thy best be true
And let each gracious thought
Show fairest counterpart in speech and deeds.

God reads the heart tis true
But faith unkept of works
Lies choked in weeds.



Yea, a man may say, Thou hast faith, and I have **works**:
shew me thy faith without thy **works**,
and I will shew thee my faith by my **works**

**James 2:18**

## JUST WAIT ON THE LORD

There are so many sorrows that we have to hear
And sometimes nobody seems to care
But some day there shall be an end
If we will just wait on the Lord.

Some times we are so burdened with sorrow
That we can't hide the tears from those we meet
But all tears shall be wiped away
If we will just wait on the Lord.

We wonder along with blinded eyes
With our heart and mind so full of distress
But we will overcome some day
If we will just wait on the Lord.

Sin is so broad in this world today
That our hearts are burdened night and day
But I know that some day there shall be an end
If we will just wait on the Lord.

written Nov. 8, 1945

## LIVE FOR SOMETHING

Live for something and live earnest
Though the work may humble be
By the world of men unnoticed
Known alone to God and thee.

Every act has priceless value
To the architect of fate
Tis the spirit of doing
That alone will make it great.

Live for something God and angels
Are thy watchers in the strife
And above the smoke and conflict
Gleams the victors crown of life.

Live for something, God has given
Freely of his stores divine
Richest gifts of earth and heaven
If thou will may be Thine.

## LONELY STAR

Be not dismayed as once again
The world is plunged in dreadful war
Judea's deathless radiance
Still gleams beyond the ramparts far.

Let bleeding hearts not lose their trust
The ways of God are not of men
The pall will lift, the grief will pass
That lonely star will shine again.

It happened many times before
A sorry world heart broken sore
By keeping faith has learned that war
Can't quench the light of Bethlehem's star.

## (MY BEST) SECOND PRIZE

I have often tried for the prizes three
By stories and poems of flowers and trees
With tales of lads and lassies gay
Stories of Christmas and New Year's Day.

Stories of sadness, stories of cheer
Stories that bought to the eyes a tear
Stories that brought to the life a smile
Thinking and working all the while.

I've racked my brain
Till it cried for rest
But I cannot stop
Till I've done my best.

## THE SMILING FOOL

If days be dark and days be blue
Though I have gained or I have lost
Oh let me to myself be true
No matter what the effort cost.

If those I meet be harsh and cruel
The words they utter proud and vain
Oh, let me be the smiling fool
And share with thee the hidden pain.

For some there are who like to wound
And be important with their sneers
God keep thou my heart attuned
With thine throughout the coming year.

Now therefore fear the LORD, and serve him
in sincerity and in **truth**:
and put away the gods which your fathers served
on the other side of the flood, and in Egypt;
and serve ye the LORD.

**Joshua 24:14**

### THE POETRY OF MARY SOUTHERS

## THROUGH THE WINDOW

As I look through the window at the clouds in the sky
Then I think of the years that have gone by
Of how we have wondered in the valley's and up life's hills steep
And of how the Dear Master keeps watch o're his sheep.

And how that we might have wandered and gone astray
If he had not watched over us night and day
But he kept watch over us with his love untold
And brought us back safely to the fold.

And how he calls us each one by name when we stray too far
And how he lets us see just where we are
Then deep down in our hearts we do rejoice
That when the Master speaks to us we know his voice.

Its wonderful to know that you're one of the sheep
Of a shepherd who never goes to sleep
But keeps watch over his sheep night and day
And sees that none of them go astray.

For he said, "my sheep know my voice
And a stranger they follow not"
So we cannot stray if we stay close to the flock
Where the good shepherd always keeps watch.

Then being one of the sheep of the fold
Who was washed in his blood of the lamb and made whole
Of the shepherd over the sheep that keeps watch of the folds
Through the windows of glory.

## *IF I COULD ONLY WRITE A LINE*

## PRACTICAL

At Christmas time when mother dear
Her various presents brings
Folks always dreamt the same old chant
She gives such practical things.

Always something that a body can use
Nothing foolish or vain
Each gift thought out and carefully planned
To a common sense refrain.

Her sister in law loves bright pretty things
Bangles bracelets and beads
So she received hem stitched towels
A thing every housewife needs.

And thus it went all down the line
No surprises to give the heart wings
Were ever known through mother dear
And her too, too practical things.

### THE POETRY OF MARY SOUTHERS

## HE SUFFERED THAT WE MIGHT LIVE

Oh if we would only realize today
What love Jesus gave to the world
When he died upon the cross on Calvary
And let his banner be unfurled.

There is no love in heaven or in earth
That was given to man that day
When Jesus suffered and died upon the cross
In such a cruel and lowly way.

Where could we find such a friend
That would give all as he did
Who nailed all our sins to the cross
And suffered and died that we might live.

Lets praise the lord with all our heart
For all the joy that earth brings
To our dear saviors who was dead and buried
But on Easter Sunday he arose again.

*IF I COULD ONLY WRITE A LINE*

## EVENING THOUGHT

If this day some heart has pained
By act of mine in cruel disdain
This day dear Jesus,
I have lived from thee
A journey apart unto eternity.

Have I pillaged in thoughtless curse
This rapture his fingers gave verdant earth
Be that held in memory stark
I saw no beauty,
I have courted the dark.

This my prayer
When life's toll is o're
May I rest in sanctuary of his grace so pure
When dust to dust I am but earth to land
He may say, "Come as created, thou have lived a man".

And when he had called the people **unto** him
with his disciples also, he said **unto** them,
Whosoever will **come** after **me**, let him deny himself,
and take up his cross, and follow **me**.

**Mark 8:34**

*THE POETRY OF MARY SOUTHERS*

## WILL HE HAVE TIME FOR YOU?

No time for God
What fools we are to clutter up
Our lives with common things
And leave without hearts gate
The lord of life and life itself our God.

No time for God
As soon to say no time
To eat or sleep or love or die
Take time for God.

Or you shall dwarf your soul
And when the angel death
Comes knocking at your door
A poor misshapen thing you'll be to step into eternity.

No time for God
That day when sickness comes
Or trouble finds you out
And you cry out for God, will he have time for you?

No time for God
Some day you'll lay aside this mortal self
And make your way to worlds unknown
And when you meet him face to face
Will he, should he, have time for you?

*IF I COULD ONLY WRITE A LINE*

## LET'S GO FORWARD!

Another great leader has fallen
But lets not stop but go forward
He was one who looked to Jesus to bear his cross
That's why that he went forward.

Its true that Jesus has kissed him to sleep
But in ou memory we shall forever keep
And Jeus himself our leader shall be
And we shall go forward.

For Jesus said, "trust me rather than man
For vain is the help of man, for man must die"
And he still lives forever on high
And we must go forward.

And he shall forever be our captain and leader too
Until all the work on earth is through
So let's you and I follow him to the end
And by his grace go forward trusting him.

As commander in chief, he was a leader indeed
God led him and he leads us
And may God's will and his will still be
And that every man shall be free.

On January 30th 1882 a great hero was born
And in 1912 he took his seat with faith in God
And after finishing his work well done, fell asleep
On April 12, 1945 to receive his reward.

In memory of President F.D. Roosevelt

written April 14, 1945

***THE POETRY OF MARY SOUTHERS***

## MY GUARDIAN ANGEL

The most wonderful thing
That has happened to me
The gift of my angel
My companion to be.

Although I can't see him
I know that he is here
God taught me his ownself
He would always be near.

To guide me and help me
Along life's treacherous way
I know I should reverence
My good angel today.

How could I in actions
Hurt something near divine
Made by God in heaven
One of his own choice mine.

To thy face dear angel
May I never bring flame
By my side keep watches
My footsteps avoid shame.


To my neighbor

## THE POWER OF GOD

What man on earth has the power of God
When he rules heaven and earth
Even the sun moon and stars obey him
The wind rain and the whole earth must obey him
Where is the power of man?

God has given man wisdom to do many things
And through their success they forget God
But when God moves in glory
All men can see the power of God.

Man has gone so far as to try to rule
The wind lightning and rain
But with all their efforts it still stands
As the power of God with his mighty hand.

King Solomon was the wisest man on earth
For God said because thou has asked for understanding
I have given thee a wise and an understanding heart
So that there was none like thee, neither after thee
Shall any arise like unto thee the power of God.

Man has thought himself so wise in many things
And they boast of knowledge and power
But when my master moves in heaven they know
That there's no power on earth like the power of God.

written April 9, 1948

***THE POETRY OF MARY SOUTHERS***

## HAS THE LIGHT GROWN DIM

Has the light grown dim
That shown so bright on Easter morn
When Jesus arose from the grave
And those wicked men was so alarmed.

When they thought that they had conquered him
When they had nailed him to the cross
And when he arose on Easter morn as the light of the world
They saw that their gain was lost.

This world is in a terrible way today
All because that their light has grown dim
And there will never be peace or light in this world of sin
Until all people shall turn to him.

Dear lord please help us to turn to you
With all our heart, soul, strength, and mind
Please help us to never let our light grow dim
For all in this world is thine.

Dear lord help us to hold our lights high
As we travel through this world each day
That others may see you shining in us
And help them to find the way and we saved.

written January 17, 1946

*IF I COULD ONLY WRITE A LINE*

## JUST JESUS AND ME

It seems sometimes that there's nothing but darkness
All around me there is no light to see
But with it all I am satisfied walking
With just Jesus and me.

For I know while walking with Jesus
There is enough light to see
And I know that I can never lose my way
With just Jesus and me.

When nights are long and dreary
And there is nothing but sorrow it seems
But when I whisper a prayer, its such relief
With just Jesus and me.

And when this life's journey is over
And there is no more in this world for me
When I get to the river of Jordan, I'll be so happy
Walking with just Jesus and me.

It may be on land or on the sea
If I stay with Jesus no harm can be
And I know that someday I shall be free
If I will only walk with just Jesus and me.

*THE POETRY OF MARY SOUTHERS*

## PROMISES OF OUR LORD

I will give them all the grace necessary
In their state of life
I will establish peace
In their houses.

I will comfort them
In all of their afflictions
I will be their secure refuge during life,
And above all in death.

I will bestow a large blessing
Upon all their undertakings
.Sinners shall find in my heart
The source and the infinite ocean of mercy.


That ye be not slothful, but followers of them who
through faith and patience inherit the **promises**

**Hebrews 6:12**

*IF I COULD ONLY WRITE A LINE*

## PETER'S BARK

Athwart the war's engulfing maw
I saw a ship at sea
A ship without a human flow
First launched in Galilee.

On Lake Genesareth's foaming wave
Twas launched by Christ the King
Who captaincy to Peter gave
And sealed it with a ring.

Two thousand years have come and gone
The earthly realms decay
Like Jose's sun in Gabon
That ship still lights the way.

The worldly leaders scorn the light
To grope in fog and sin
Their trust they put in force and might
That prods the beast within.

Their conquests shall be set at naught
Their marshaled hast dispersed
The victory with bloodshed bought
Is in the end accursed.

The bark of Peter rides the waves
Its pennants all unfurled
Its light alone has power to save
A fog enshrouded world.

*THE POETRY OF MARY SOUTHERS*

## THE VALLEY OF HUMILIATION

When everything in life goes wrong
And cares are multiplied
And sorrow takes from you your song
And with heartache you've cried.

When you've tried to do your best
And failure you now face
And shame does seem so cruel a test
For you in life's short race.

When friends forsake and friendless you
Hopes for a cheering word
And sorrows come again anew
But no kind word is heard.

When grief and sadness fill your soul
Your heart does mourn and bleed
You long and pray to be made whole
And cry out in great need.

Fear not my sister, only pray
Gethsemane is near
For we must face it in this way
Have courage, do not fear..

The son of God has gone before
He first this price did pray
He will with you remain the more
Hold fast till break of day.

When you with one eternal yes
Have said, "thy will be done"
He will forever your soul bless
And strength to bear the cross he'll give.

*IF I COULD ONLY WRITE A LINE*

## WHEN WILL I KNOW

I do not know or can I tell
When the face of Christ I shall see
But I am sure, and I know so well
One of these days I am going home.

When will I see and how can I tell
What mine eyes some day shall see
And I am sure to live with Jesus
Oh how happy I will be.

When will I know, how can I tell
When he calls me to my home above
Redeemed through his atoning blood
I am sheltered in my Savior's love.


It is well, yes, with my soul, I know
And the gates sstand ajar for me
To give an entrance to that city fair
Where loved ones are waiting for me there.

***THE POETRY OF MARY SOUTHERS***

# *CHAPTER FOURTEEN*

# *MOTHER, FATHER & CHILDREN*

## THANKFUL FOR MOTHER

Lord how thankful
We are to say
That we have mother dear with us
This mother's day.

May we love and cherish her
Along life's way
And be a blessing to her we pray.

For whosoever shall do the will of God,
the same is my brother, and my sister, and **mother**.

**Mark 3:35**

***IF I COULD ONLY WRITE A LINE***

## THE ARMS OF MOTHER EARTH

The mother of all mother
Is mother earth
For God himself made our first mother
Out of mother earth.

And as a mother holds out her hands
For her child at birth
So does mother earth hold out her arms
For her children's return.

For we must go back
To the arms of mother earth.
It matters not where that we may be
On the land or the sea.

Oh Jesus please have mercy
and stand by me
For I must go back to mother earth.

You may run away from mother
And go to the end of the world
But it matters not where you go or what you do
You must return to the arm's of mother earth

written April 30 1944

## FATHER'S PRIDE

Just a wee lad was he
But as sweet as could be
His father's pride and joy
Was this dear little boy.

Each morn he'd whisper sweet
"Tis' time to rise from sleep"
And then he'd cuddle near
To me he was so dear.

But when he hurt his knee
He would not come to me
To his mother he'd run
Dear little chap, my son.

## MOTHER

I've trudged in vain the weary mile
I've hungered for the sight of you
It was the memory of your smile
That brought me home to mother true.

What if your hair is as white as snow
And that your brow is furrowed too
I guess that we sons ought to know
We placed them there with things we do.

I love her more than can be told
There's nothing finer on this sod
Than saintly mothers who are old
For then they are so near to God.

*IF I COULD ONLY WRITE A LINE*

## LITTLE BROTHER

I must answer little brother
For he seems to think it odd
That our lady is our mother
And the mother of our God.

So I tell the simple story
Of the babe of Bethlehem
And of how hallowed glory
Shines in Mary's diadem.

Little brother loved our mother
And his heart is filled with joy
As we picture to each other
How our lady loved her boy.

But he's very close to crying
As the story I recall
How the word made flesh when dying
How his mother to us all.

Then we smile and greet each other
With an understanding nod
For you see our own dear mother
We have given back to God.

*THE POETRY OF MARY SOUTHERS*

## MOTHER OF JESUS

Why is thy face so lit with smiles
Mother of Jesus why
And wherefore is thy beaming look
So fixed upon the sky.

Mother how canst thou smile today
How can thine eyes be bright
When he thy son, thy life, thy all
Hath vanished from thy sight.

His rising form on Olivet
A summer's shadow cast
The branches of the hoary tree
Draped as the shadows passed.

And as he rose with all his train
Of righteous souls around
His blessings fell into thy heart
Like dew upon the ground.

Oh why do not thy hands detain
His feet upon their way?
Oh why doth not the mother speak
And bid her son to stay?

Ah no thy love is rightful love
From all self-seeking free
The change that is such gain to him.

*IF I COULD ONLY WRITE A LINE*

## LEAN UPON MY ARM MOTHER

Pray lean upon my arm mother
Your form is feeble now
And silvery are the locks that shade
The furrows on thy brow.

Your step is not so strong mother
As in the days gone by
But strong as ever is the love
That beams within your eye.

When I was a babe, mother
With tender love inspired
You carried us for many an hour
Until yours arms were tired.

From childhood up to manhood's years
Through every pain and ill
You watched me with a loving eye
You watch my welfare still.

And shall I fail you now, mother
When all your strength has fled
Neglect to guide your feeble steps
As through life's vale you tread.

Your eyes are dim with age mother
Care lines are on your brow
The little feet you guided once
Are strong to guide you now.

Then lean upon my arms mother
Henceforth lifes going through
What you did so long for him
Your boy will do for you.

***THE POETRY OF MARY SOUTHERS***

# IN MEMORY
# SHE SERVED THE LORD
# IN WORD AND DEED

Our lives are oft time darkened
Our eyes with tears are dim
And we mourn for our dear loved one
Who has gone to Christ the king.

We miss her deeds of kindness
Her words so full of love
Which led many a precious soul
To seek the Lord above.

We miss her hand to guide us
Her words to cheer us on
Words that help us keep the pathway
In the race we have begun.

We shall miss her as we journey
In life's pathway here below
But we know she's with our savior
Where there is no sin or woe.

For her life was hid in Jesus
And her hope was fired above
She was on her way to heaven
And was happy in his love.

*IF I COULD ONLY WRITE A LINE*

## MOTHER

How precious is the name mother
She is a blessing sent from God
She understands and loves you
As no one but God and she will do.

For as Jesus told John, behold thy mother
When they had nailed him to the cross
For he loved and honored his mother
And he did not forget her while dying on the cross.

No other name is so sweet as mother
For it is next to the blessed name of Christ
For she'll guide us through all life's sorrows
And Jesus will lead us to paradise.

Just as the mother of Jesus
Who followed her dear son to the cross
So Will our dear mother love us
And lead us to the cross.

Dear Lord we thank thee today
For our dear mother that you gave
That by her love and teaching of thee
Our souls shall be saved.


written April 30th 1944

### THE POETRY OF MARY SOUTHERS

## DEAREST MOTHER

Dear mother while thinking of you
My heart over flows with love
And how grateful I am to you mother dear
That you taught me of God above.

And at your knee dear mother
You taught mw how to pray
You taught me to look too Jesus
For he's the only way.

Oh how I think you dear mother
For since you've gone away
I've had many a trial and sorrow
But I haven't forgot to pray.

For Jesus has been mother and father
To me he's my only stay
How grateful I am to you dear mother
That you taught me how to pray.

Every since you left me mother dear
Through all my doubts and fears
I put all my trust in Jesus
And mother he seems to be so near.

I'm looking ever to Jesus mother
And holding fast to his unchanging hand
And some day I'll see you dear mother
In that blessed promised land.

May God bless you in heaven dear mother
On this mothers day
Again I thank you mother dear
That you taught me how to pray.

*IF I COULD ONLY WRITE A LINE*

## MOTHER'S DAY

I love the words perhaps because
When I was leaving mother
Standing at last in solemn pause
We looked at one another.

And I saw in mother's eyes
The love she could not tell me
A love eternal as the skies
Whatever fate befell me.

She put her arms around my neck
And soothed the pain of leaving
And though her heart was like to break
She spoke no word of grieving.

She let no tear bedim her eyes
For fear that might distress me
But kissing me she said goodbye
And asked my God to bless me.

***THE POETRY OF MARY SOUTHERS***

## DEAR MOTHER

Dear mother oh how much I do miss you today
I haven't the words to say
I miss your smiling face so much
And those sweet and tender words you used to say.

I miss those words of courage and tender love
That will always live within my heart
Until I shall meet you dear mother
In that land where we shall nevermore part.

Sleep on in peace, dear mother, and take your rest
From the toil and trials of this world
May the Lord help us to live as you did mother
And let his banner be unfurled.

On this mother's day, mother dear
Everything seems so empty without you
But God's will has been done
And by his grace someday we will see you again
In that blessed promised land.


written Mother's Day May 5th, 1945

*IF I COULD ONLY WRITE A LINE*

## BLESS THOU ME OH MOTHER

Bless thou me oh mother
Bless thou me thy child
Thee I call no other
Virgin mother mild.

Bless thou thoughts and actions
All the livelong day
Keep me from distractions
When I try to pray.

Bless thou too oh mother
All the friends I love
Father, mother, brother
And the ones above.

Lay thy hands in blessings
On the whole wide earth
Tenderly caressing
The hand that gives me birth.

Bless thou us oh mother
When our work is done
And the angels whisper
It is time to come.

May we be awakened
By thy lily hand
And by thee be taken
To the promised land.

***THE POETRY OF MARY SOUTHERS***

*IF I COULD ONLY WRITE A LINE*

## THE POETRY OF MARY SOUTHERS

*IF I COULD ONLY WRITE A LINE*

An Old Louisville School tablet used by Mary Southers

Assorted writing tablets used by Mary Southers

Copy of letter to Mary Southers

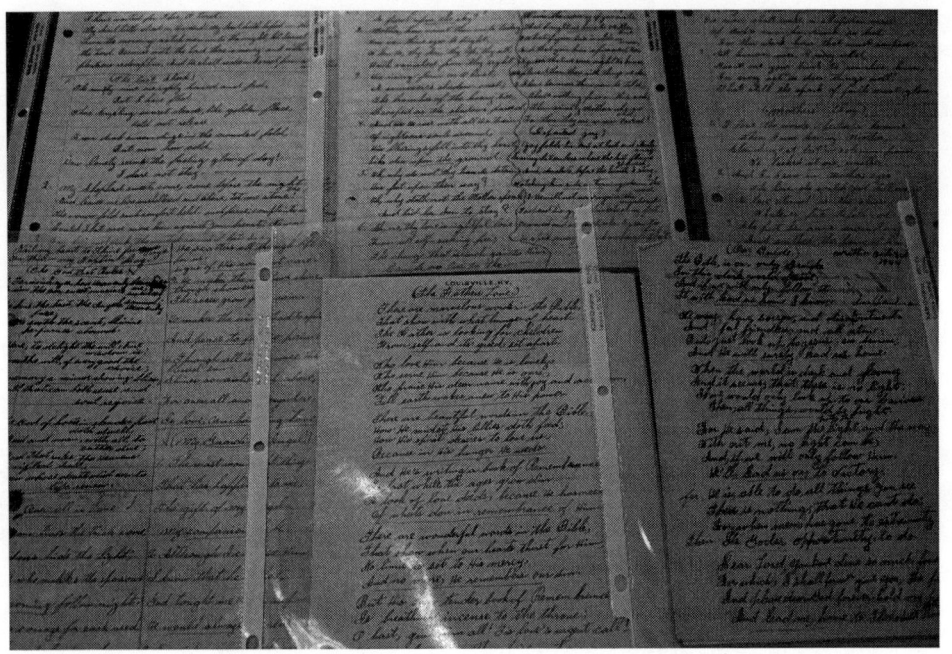

Handwritten pages of Mary Southers poetry